"*Wicca's Charm* is one of those books that charms and beguiles you even as it informs you. The reporting is seamless and the writing effortless. Catherine Sanders has made a brilliant debut as a writer on a spiritual matter that should be of deep interest to all thinking Americans."

—DAVID AIKMAN, former senior correspondent for *Time* magazine, and author of *Jesus in Beijing, A Man of Faith: The Spiritual Journey of George W. Bush,* and the novel *Qi*

"For Christians who want to understand the culture our own failures have sown and are now reaping, and for those who want to reach out persuasively to this emerging culture, Sanders's warm, clear, and helpful introduction to W

g

"Catherine   espect-
ful. It will   it will
also allow   deeper
insight int

"Catherin   honest
journey in   ade an
erudite co 4x808 ✓1008   t."

—LILIAN CALLES BARGER, author of *Eve's Revenge: Women and a Spirituality of the Body,* and founder of the Damaris Project

"*Wicca's Charm* is a *must*-read for parents! A fascinating account full of stories and personal interviews, Catherine Sanders's book provides wonderful insights into why young people seek alternative spiritualities and what Christians should know about it!"

—SUSAN ALEXANDER YATES, best-selling author of several books, including, *And Then I Had Teenagers: Encouragement for Parents of Teens and Preteens*

"*Wicca's Charm* is a fine demonstration of a rare Christian virtue: attentive listening. With a clear conviction that authentic Christian belief is a valid response to Wiccan yearnings, Sanders holds, in tension, a humble recognition that Christian compromise with materialistic rationalism and individualism in Western culture has driven many to take up dangerous alternatives."

—PETER HARRIS, director of A Rocha International

"*Wicca's Charm* provides an accessible, thorough, and sensitive guide to understanding contemporary interest in Wicca and neo-Paganism. It will be of help to anyone interested in understanding how nature worship under various names is reasserting itself in the Western world."

—JAMES A. HERRICK, professor of communication at Hope College, and author of *The Making of the New Spirituality: The Eclipse of the Western Religious Tradition*

"Catherine Sanders spent more than a year listening to Wiccans in an attempt to understand the growth and appeal of Wicca today. She encourages Christians to dialogue with neo-Pagans, clarifying points of common ground while simultaneously pointing out with compassion and sensitivity the inadequacies of Paganism to fulfill their deep and legitimate longings."

—MARDI KEYES, codirector of L'Abri Fellowship in Southborough, Massachusetts, and author of *Feminism and the Bible*

Wicca's Charm

UNDERSTANDING *the* SPIRITUAL HUNGER BEHIND
the RISE *of* MODERN WITCHCRAFT
and PAGAN SPIRITUALITY

CATHERINE
EDWARDS SANDERS

SHAW BOOKS
an imprint of WATERBROOK PRESS

Wicca's Charm
A SHAW BOOK
PUBLISHED BY WATERBROOK PRESS
12265 Oracle Boulevard, Suite 200
Colorado Springs, Colorado 80921
A division of Random House, Inc.

All Scripture quotations, unless otherwise indicated, are taken from the *Holy Bible, New International Version*®. NIV®. Copyright © 1973, 1978, 1984 by International Bible Society. Used by permission of Zondervan Publishing House. All rights reserved.

Some names have been changed to protect the identities of the persons involved.

ISBN 0-87788-198-7

SHAW BOOKS and its aspen leaf logo are registered trademarks of WaterBrook Press, a division of Random House, Inc.

Library of Congress Cataloging-in-Publication Data
Sanders, Catherine Edwards.
    Wicca's Charm : understanding the spiritual hunger behind the rise of modern witchcraft and pagan spirituality / by Catherine Edwards Sanders.—1st ed.
        p. cm.
    "A Shaw Book"
    Includes bibliographical references.
    ISBN 0-87788-198-7 (alk. paper)
    1. Witchcraft. 2. Occultism—Religious aspects—Christianity. 3. Christianity and other religions—Neopaganism. 4. Neopaganism—Relations—Christianity. I. Title.
BR115.O3S26 2005
261.2'994—dc22

                                                                              2005015526

Printed in the United States of America
2005—First Edition

10 9 8 7 6 5 4 3 2 1

To Wallace, with love and devotion,
and in memory of
Sue Tucker Yates (1907–2005)

Contents

Acknowledgments

In the course of researching and writing this book, there were times I never really thought I would reach the point of writing acknowledgments. Many people helped me get here, but first and foremost I must thank Tom Phillips and the generosity of the Phillips Foundation for providing me not only with funding for this project but with encouragement and moral support along the way. Special thanks go to John Farley, Jeff Hollingsworth, and Claudia Winkler for their early reading of the manuscript and their support during my fellowship year.

I am grateful to all the people I interviewed and met with while writing this book. Tal Brooke and his staff at the Spiritual Counterfeits Project provided me with a warm welcome to northern California. Brooks Alexander was a wonderful resource, and I thank him for letting me accompany him during his own research. Thanks to Sara and Brian in Worcester, Massachusetts, for opening their home and lives to me. I am grateful to Jennifer Goodson for her support and for introducing me to Lilian Calles Barger and the Damaris Project. Thanks to Lilian for her encouragement on this project. Thanks also to Kristen Bucher for her continued interest and for going with me to southwest Virginia on that rainy day in May.

All those who provided me with a place to research and write were gracious and generous. Thanks to Tim Keefer, Bill and Robin Fetsch, and Connie Elliot, and to Lynn Gibson for a retreat in the city.

The C. S. Lewis Institute provided me with wonderful teaching and sound biblical scholarship while I wrote. I appreciate the efforts and work

ACKNOWLEDGMENTS

of those at the Institute and am grateful for the encouragement of Tom
Tarrants and Art Lindsley. I am also grateful to Os Guinness for his encouragement during the writing and to Frederica Mathewes-Green for telling
me that she knew the right agent for this project. She was right!

Everyone at WaterBrook Press gave me a very warm welcome. I am
grateful to my agent, Kathy Helmers, and to Don Pape, formerly of Water-
Brook Press, for his immediate enthusiasm for my project. My editor, Elisa
Stanford, provided great support during our intense editing period. All
three of you "got" this book from the beginning, and it was such a breath
of fresh air. The production team at WaterBrook did a wonderful job. Any
errors in the book are my own.

I am grateful to all my wonderful friends who supported the book and
prayed for me as I wrote—you know who you are.

My family sustained me through the writing with their listening ears
and support. Thanks to my parents, Tony and Toler Edwards; my brother,
Graham, and his wife, Joanna; and my sister, Elizabeth, who read some
early chapters and was enthusiastic about my writing. Thanks also to the
Sanders family, whose support has been invaluable.

I especially want to thank my precious grandmother, Sue Tucker Yates,
who died at ninety-seven just before I finished the book. Her excitement
and enthusiasm for this book were always high, and I only wish she could
have seen the finished product.

Lastly, I want to thank my wonderful husband, Wallace, who put up
with my being sequestered for many weekends, did more than his fair share
of chores while I wrote, gave up many hours of his time to read the manuscript, and provided incredible critique and helpful edits. He made me lots
of cups of tea without being asked, and he also willingly spent late nights
at the library for me helping verify sources while he himself had a heavy
workload. His enthusiasm, interest, love, and support sustained me.

PREFACE

M y place in society has become so altered. I work, I contribute, but I have become invisible," a woman laments to a friend. A mother of grown children who works as a nurse, the woman has just had a hysterectomy. She uses ritual in a small outdoor ceremony to deal with feelings of loss after the surgery and to seek direction. After taking off her clothes, she covers herself with red-clay rune symbols* and buries the organs removed from surgery in part of her wedding dress. She and her friend perform a Wiccan ritual. They both play flutes and place crystals and a feather on the burial spot.[1]

In another corner of America, a chestnut-haired seventeen-year-old sits at the Starbucks inside a popular bookstore chain in Charlotte, North Carolina. Deana and her blonde friend, Ellen, share a large coffee and discuss how they became Wiccans. Deana's parents regularly attend a local Presbyterian church and have sent her to church camp since she was a young child. They don't know she practices witchcraft. Her mother thinks she is Buddhist, and she says her father just gets angry that she doesn't like going to church.

"After I read the book about love spells, what really began to attract me was that Wicca respects nature, that God is in nature, that it focuses on protecting the environment, and that it empowers women," she says.

The girls take drugs, perform Wiccan rituals, and celebrate Wiccan

---

* *A note on terminology:* I explain terms like these throughout the book, but I have also included expanded definitions in the glossary.

holidays. They tell me that their behavior would cause alarm among most students at their high school, but they see themselves as progressive—breaking new religious ground.

"A revolution can take place slowly," says the blonde. "I don't think we will see a mass movement toward Wicca, but slowly over time it is going to become a regular part of the culture."*

ASKING QUESTIONS

I first encountered Wicca as a magazine reporter. During an editorial meeting one September, I was asked to write a piece about Halloween, and soon the conversation turned to Wicca. My editor's questions might be yours: "What is the deal with all those TV shows that feature teenage witches?" "Is interest in witchcraft a growing trend?" On that Friday afternoon he asked me to find answers for him and write a short article about Wicca.

When I stopped at the bookstore to purchase a book on Wicca, I was stunned at the variety of books to choose from. I wondered who these people were that practiced Wicca and whether I should be wary of them. At the time, when I heard the term *Wicca,* I thought, *Oh, Wiccans are those scary people who are part of a cult and worship the devil.* In a reflective moment I might have singled out a few kids in high school who wore black all the time—they might have been Wiccans.

When I began my research, I started to meet many people who called themselves witches, and at first they unnerved me. I wasn't used to meeting people who claim to cast spells; it all sounded rather sinister. But as I

---

* Undocumented quotes such as this one are from personal interviews conducted by the author and used by permission or from statements made by individuals in public venues.

began to meet and talk with both young and older Wiccans, I found that their involvement with Wicca was not at the beckoning of some cultlike leader. My stereotypes of these people soon began to embarrass me, and my curiosity propelled me to do more research. I would soon find out that Wicca could no longer be characterized as a bizarre, marginal religion. As I began to understand in the bookstore, it is a widespread and increasingly popular spiritual practice.

PROMPTING DIALOGUE

Neo-Paganism—which includes the modern practice of witchcraft also known as Wicca—is an overarching term for earth-based spirituality incorporating nature worship through a revival of the polytheistic worship of ancient gods and goddesses. Wicca is also known as "the Craft," and most Wiccans believe in the manipulation of the supernatural through rite, ritual, and spell casting. In 1986 a federal court of appeals (*Dettmer v. Landon*) ruled that "The Church of Wicca" was to be recognized constitutionally as a religion.

It is difficult to gauge the numbers involved in neo-Paganism. People can be reluctant to identify themselves as neo-Pagan, and many enter and leave neo-Paganism without ever being counted. One Wiccan I spoke to told me she guessed there are 5 million adherents. Covenant of the Goddess—the oldest and largest interdenominational organization of witches in the United States*—estimates from a 1999 poll that there are almost

---

* Wiccans have traditionally organized themselves according to the different types of witchcraft they practice—somewhat equivalent to Christian denominations. But those distinctions are becoming less pronounced as more young people practice Wicca on their own or don't observe any particular tradition or practice.

800,000 Wiccans and Pagans in America.[2] Perhaps more accurate would be the estimation of sociologist Helen Berger, who spent ten years as a participant and observer of the neo-Pagan community. She estimates that in 1999 there were between 150,000 and 200,000 Pagans;[3] it's likely there are many more today. Berger's census revealed that California has the highest percentage of neo-Pagans at 15.7 percent, followed by New York and Massachusetts at 7.3 percent and 7.6 percent, respectively.[4]

By Covenant of the Goddess's estimates, female witches outnumber males two to one in the United States, and much of the recent growth among Wiccans has been among women. These figures, however, do not include the growing segment of the population who would agree with most neo-Pagan beliefs but would not identify themselves as neo-Pagan. The number of adherents is constantly in flux, but as we will see later, there are other ways to gauge the growing interest in neo-Paganism.

One neo-Pagan Web site lists nine thousand covens on its site. A coven is a group of people who convene for religious, magic, or psychic purposes; it usually refers to a meeting of witches. Covens range from a gathering in which witches are systematically taught about magic to a coffee klatsch of like-minded Pagans.* Some witches meet in covens, while others are solitary practitioners.

You may have the same fears and questions about neo-Paganism and Wicca that I did when I began my research. What may surprise you is that Wiccans are just as likely to be in Topeka, Kansas, as in San Francisco, California. They may very well be living in your neighborhood.

You may also be surprised to learn that Wiccans and neo-Pagans are

---

* Refers to the religion of Paganism or the modern practitioners of this religion. When the term is lowercased (pagan), it refers to ancient pagan peoples or pagan practices.

among the more fascinating people I have met. Their wonder at life, its rhythms, and the unspeakable beauty of nature is something we can all learn from in our crazy, fast-paced world. Many dance to the beat of their own drum, like it that way, and revel in their eccentricities.

Indeed, most of the people I met while writing this book would not fit common pointy-hatted, green-faced stereotypes. The witch in the Dairy Queen, whom you will meet later, provided me with fascinating insight into the Wiccan subculture. You'll also meet a brilliant academic who moved to Greece because she felt marginalized by academia. You'll meet a sixteen-year-old student at one of America's top private schools who says that Wicca is the only thing that makes sense to her. You'll read why a former witch in Salem, Massachusetts, embraced the gospel message. You'll encounter a well-known author who grew up in the Christian church but couldn't find her place there. And you'll read about the Princeton University student who flirted with Wicca but became a Christian while studying in Spain.

It is never easy being an outsider writing about other people's spirituality. As a Christian I can never see Wicca from the inside because there are limits on how much I can participate. I cannot invoke their spirits or take part in their rituals. And so I am grateful to all of the Wiccans I encountered for telling me their stories.

When I started my research, I wanted to interview Wiccans exclusively. But as anyone who has spent time within the neo-Pagan community knows, it is a diverse group. Where there are Wiccans, there are eclectic Pagans or Goddess worshipers. (*Eclectic Paganism* draws on a variety of pagan symbols and rituals to create a spirituality, while *Goddess worship* is a form of neo-Pagan spirituality whose practitioners worship the Mother Goddess only; in America, Goddess worship is largely rooted in feminism.) And the list could go on.

So although I have titled this book *Wicca's Charm*, I have included interviews with Pagans of all different stripes. I have not attempted to cover every aspect of Wicca, let alone provide a comprehensive view of neo-Paganism. If I had, this book would never have been written. Wicca's flexible principles differ from one practitioner to the next, so I have tried to describe these different spiritual practices as I encountered them. I refer to practitioners of Wicca as Wiccans or witches, depending on the preferences of those I interviewed. I also use the terms neo-Pagan and Pagan interchangeably.

My own interest in Wicca stems from a desire as a journalist and as a Christian to understand why Wicca attracts people. My Christian convictions and participation in the Christian community prompted me to see whether people turned to Wicca because they perceived Christianity as a patriarchal and dogmatic religion or whether they had burned out on Christian culture, particularly evangelical culture. I was surprised to discover that even if I didn't ask any questions about the church, Wiccans always mentioned it. After a while I asked everyone I met about their impressions of the Christian church and faith.

As we'll see, I found that Wicca speaks to those interested not only in the supernatural but also in environmental causes and feminism—issues that are all too often neglected by American churches. Many of these seekers are looking for a spirituality that addresses these issues.

I don't believe witchcraft is the answer to the struggle these seekers are facing, but the Christian church hasn't exactly offered a welcoming alternative for them to consider, although the gospel message itself offers them great hope and answers to their questions. Sadly, rather than reaching out in love, as Scripture commands, to those who are different from those within the church and who may be seeking spirituality through Wicca or Paganism, the church seems desperate to protect and distance itself from such people. But pulling up the drawbridge and lobbing arrows at Wiccans from the parapets of Christendom just drives people away. Yet out of fear and ignorance, many Christians have refused to engage in dialogue with a Wiccan family member, neighbor, or friend. *Wicca's Charm* is not only an exploration of Wicca in America but a reflection on how Christians treat Wiccans and Pagans.

This book chronicles what I saw and heard as I spent a year researching and talking with people. My background as a reporter—a journalist's-eye view—has guided me in telling the story of how and why Wicca has become popular in today's society. My beliefs as a Christian have guided me in finding out why many people are drawn to Wicca and bypass the church. My hope is that this book will help Christians and Wiccans alike understand what divides them, will prompt a dialogue between Christians and seekers, and will speak truth into Wicca's confusing belief system. I invite Wiccans to join in the journey as well and read this book with an open mind.

As a parent, you may have picked up this book hoping to learn more about your teenager's recent decision to practice Wicca. As a Christian, you may want to have a better understanding of why a Wiccan friend is more drawn to witchcraft than the church. (Some of you may simply be curious about Wicca.) As a spiritual seeker, you may want to know some of the background of both Christianity and Wiccan spirituality. In the end, my desire is for you to become better informed about this spirituality that has come to the fore at this time in history. Our culture has tilled the soil, making it fertile enough for the seeds of Wicca to grow. This may be of concern to some, and for others, cause to celebrate. But to dismiss this spirituality as fringe or something practiced by an insignificant minority group would be to miss the point of what is really happening in our society.

MODEL BEHAVIOR

The fact that I was writing this book caused all sorts of odd reactions among my friends and family members. Most of them were rather concerned about me—"You're writing a book on *what?*" I know some people must have thought I was really strange, especially as I met with Wiccans in a variety of settings during my research.

Despite these varied reactions, I took comfort in the story of the apostle Paul at Mars Hill in Athens in ancient Greece. He waded into the pool of pagan thought and religion. And he spent time there. He complimented the religious zeal of the pagan Athenians as he walked by their temples and idols. He knew their literature. His words and actions were so intriguing to the pagan Greeks that they invited him to speak at Mars Hill, a place of honor where new ideas were exchanged and challenged. Paul knew Greek literature so well that he quoted from their own pagan poets to explain the gospel. The line that Christians know—"In him we live and move and have our being" (Acts 17:28)—is straight from the mouth of the pagan poet Epimenides who lived in Crete in the sixth century BC. This would have been very familiar to Paul's audience.

This scriptural account of Paul in Athens enables us to freely embrace truth in any form, wherever it is found. Paul's precedent of quoting pagan poets empowers Christians to do the same and indicates that morsels of truth and insights from general revelation may be found in non-Christian sources. If you were to follow Paul's approach when talking with a Pagan teen today, for example, you might quote a line from the well-known neo-Pagan Wiccan writer Starhawk. But it takes time to read Starhawk's *The Spiral Dance* and see how her yearnings can be met by a relationship with

Christ. How astonishing that seems: An ancient equivalent of Starhawk was quoted in the Bible!

One starting point in responding to the growth of Wicca is thoughtful confrontation with the issues it raises: What are our responsibilities to one another, to other living things, to the health of the planet? What is our place in the cosmos? Where do justice and human dignity come from? Is Wicca all that different from Christianity or spirituality in general?

You may also be asking how Wicca is different from Satanism. You may want to know why your loved one is Wiccan and what you can do about it. I grappled with such questions as I learned more about Wiccan history and practice and talked with people across the country. As you read their stories and grapple with these same questions, I hope you will find some helpful answers.

—I—

SALEM

What Is Wicca?

I n the dimly lighted room, rock music played softly and stage smoke filled the air, creating the illusion of mist. In the middle of the floor, a small altar was draped in a dark-colored cloth. Lying on the altar were candles, a wooden stick, and a dagger. A woman no older than twenty-five, dressed in black with a silver pentacle around her neck, hovered in front of the altar. Fifteen curious onlookers knelt in front of her as she began casting her spell.

She walked around the room, creating what she called "sacred space," chanting and, after each phrase, saying in a loud voice, "So mote it be!"

"Cleanse our hearts from hate and fear; fill them with love, joy, and mirth!" she said, and then she asked if the audience had any wishes, any desires. Murmurs of "good health" and "peace" filtered through the air as she wrote down the wishes.

"As witches, we call upon nature to aid us," she said loudly. She then called upon the elements of earth, fire, air, water, and spirit. After all the requests were taken, she burned in the flame of the candle the pieces of paper on which they were written, offering them up to the Goddess. The spell was cast. As the air cleared and the stage smoke filtered out the door, I lingered to speak with the young woman who had cast the spell. She smiled at me as she fingered the pentacle around her neck.

She told me that she had first visited Salem, Massachusetts, as a child and had been enchanted by the city and fascinated with witchcraft. She also felt solidarity with the women executed there for witchcraft in 1692 and was sorry for how they had been treated. As she grew up, she was delighted to discover that there were people who practiced witchcraft as a religion, and she began to practice neo-Pagan witchcraft—or Wicca—on her own. She found great meaning in her spiritual path and took part in the spell-casting demonstration to educate the public about the true nature of witchcraft. As we spoke, the audience filed out of the room into daylight in the city of Salem on Halloween.

I was part of a group of tourists who had just paid to watch a spell casting performed by women who call themselves witches. It took place in a vacant warehouse next to the haunted house that has been a tourist attraction in Salem for years. Every year since 1996 a group of witches has rented space in this warehouse from the owners of the haunted house to educate the public about witchcraft through what they call the Witch Village tour. Witches from all over the country join in to create elaborate stage sets, complete with cauldrons and old brooms, where lectures and rituals take place.

Salem was the first, if predictable, place I visited during my research for the book. The memory of Salem's history filled my mind as I wandered through the town. Tourists curious about the trials have flocked to Salem for years. Cashing in on its notoriety, the town dubs itself "Witch City." Despite the tourists, Salem is a serious pilgrimage site for many Wiccans. At Halloween, they flock to the Massachusetts town in droves to meet other Wiccans and Pagans.

Witchcraft, after all, is the stock in trade of Salem, where the lampposts are decorated with wrought-iron witches on brooms. In the gift shops, among the knickknacks and postcards, are books about the Salem witch trials that took place in the late 1600s. In almost every shop, next to these histories, are books about contemporary witchcraft—Wicca or the Craft. They were added in recent years, a sales clerk says, because they are popular and sell well.

Salem's history is one of a kind, but the growing interest in witchcraft is part of a larger cultural phenomenon. Check out the nearest metaphysical or occult shop that sells Wiccan ritual tools, apparel, books, herbs, oils, altars, incense, and even kits containing modeling clay with instructions for shaping your own goddess. The presence of these shops reflects the nation-wide growth of neo-Paganism, which includes the modern practice of witchcraft or Wicca.

WHERE DOES NEO-PAGANISM COME FROM?

Every country in the world had at some point in history its own indigenous pagan religious practices. The United States has Native American spirituality, for instance. In Ireland, the ancient Celtic spiritual leaders were Druids. In Scandinavia, the Norse gods and goddesses represented different aspects of nature. Wicca is different. It is not an indigenous religious practice unique to the British Isles, though it originated in England. In fact, it was cobbled together from various sources during the twentieth century. Scholars agree that the man responsible for most of it was a British civil servant by the name of Gerald Gardner. In the 1940s and 1950s, using ancient gods and goddesses, ideas about nature worship, and magic, Gardner and a few friends crafted their own new form of Paganism and called it Wicca.

For decades after its arrival in America in the middle of the twentieth century, neo-Pagan witchcraft was practiced only by those on the fringes of society. Yet according to Wiccan priestess Phyllis Curott, Wicca is growing

faster than any other religion in America today.[1] Since Gardner first introduced Wicca, many Wiccans have developed their own traditions of the
Craft. People from all walks of life—from teenagers to college students to
feminists to antiglobalization activists to the rather ordinary lady down the
street—consider Wicca an alternative to other mainline religions, including Christianity. The question on everyone's lips, including many neo-
Pagans, is why? Why has Wicca—long viewed as a rather odd occult fringe
movement—not only grown but crept into the mainstream?

A Religion That Defies Description

It is difficult to describe Wiccan beliefs comprehensively. This is part of its
appeal—each practitioner can add and subtract beliefs at will. Anne Niven,
editor in chief of *newWitch* magazine, told an MSNBC interviewer, "If you
ask three witches to describe their beliefs, you'll probably get about four
answers."[2] Nonetheless, I will attempt to outline the most common Wiccan
beliefs.

A Religion of Ritual
Most neo-Pagans don't articulate what they believe in tidy little sentences,
but if you listen to them long enough, their overarching philosophy en-
compasses the following four tenets:

1. All is one—Wiccans hold the monistic and pantheistic beliefs
   that all living things are of equal value. Humans have no special
   place, nor are they made in God's image. They have, for example, the same value as flowers, trees, or grass. The cosmos is
   undifferentiated universal energy, and everything is one vast
   interconnected process.

2. You are divine—Wiccans believe that they possess divine power within themselves and that they are gods or goddesses.

3. Personal power is unlimited—Wiccans believe that their power is not limited by a deity, as in Christianity.

4. Consciousness can and should be altered through the practice of rite and ritual—Wiccans believe in the supernatural realm and the practice of altered consciousness through rite, ritual, and spell casting in which they tap into the power and energy of the unseen spirit world.

Aidan Kelly is a former Wiccan who abandoned his Pagan practices to return to Roman Catholicism. He has written about the antiauthoritarian nature of the Craft and its antidogmatic approach. He writes, "No one has to believe anything.... There is no authority in the Craft outside each coven.... It's a religion of ritual rather than theology."[3]

The experience of spiritual reality is of utmost importance to Wiccans. Truth, or a body of knowledge, is less important to them. In short, the only orthodox thing about Wicca is that it has no orthodoxy. Wicca has no central book that details its beliefs, and there are no central doctrines or body of knowledge to which Wiccans adhere. Wicca tends to define itself in opposition to issues such as environmental degradation, the perceived patriarchy within Christianity, or monotheism in general.

Wicca benefits from our consumer-oriented society. It can be molded and shaped to fit the spiritual consumer's desire for experience. Instead of accepting a revealed truth, Wiccan seekers create their own truth and reality. And despite the ways technology, such as the Internet, has benefited the Wiccan community, Wicca also benefits from an anti-technological backlash and people's nostalgic yearnings for a simpler time.

Good and Evil

Wiccans have no belief in absolute good and absolute evil, which explains why they disavow Satan, whom they view as part of the Christian tradition. They acknowledge that bad things can happen, that evil exists, but they don't believe that it exists as a result of the presence of Satan. This may sound strange to Christian ears, but as studies have shown, six out of ten Americans don't believe in the person of Satan—only that he is a symbol of evil.[4]

When I tell Christians about Wicca's view of Satan, I'm almost always met with a confused reaction. I can tell what they're thinking: *Of course they worship Satan. If they are worshiping a supernatural being other than Christ, they are worshiping Satan.* One person argued with me for a good ten minutes about this. She never got the point I was trying to make: Wiccans are, as a rule, not consciously or deliberately worshiping Satan. Whether they are *unconsciously* worshiping him is an issue on which Wiccans will differ with Christians. What I did find is that those who searched for spiritual reality and missed finding it in the church often embraced the occult, intentionally or not. *Occult* literally means "hidden," which is why it is used to refer to a spirituality in which unseen forces are worshiped. Not one Wiccan I met denied the spiritual reality of what he or she believes or that frightening things can occur when Wicca is practiced. But Wiccans believe that through their own powers or by corralling the powers of the universe, they can control the evil forces that exist in the world, which, they believe, are the result of human actions.

In contrast, by nature of who they worship, Satan worshipers are deliberately and maliciously against the church and might engage in such practices as animal sacrifice. Satan worshipers may call themselves witches, but they are not neo-Pagans. Neo-Pagans have a deep reverence for the earth, and most would not want to bring harm to animals or anything else in nature. (If you have picked up this book because your child or someone you know is involved in violence against animals or other living things, I suggest you contact a pastor, a licensed counselor, or the Spiritual Counterfeits Project [listed in the resource section] for help.)

People who practice Wicca no more believe in Satan than a Buddhist does. Satan is simply not in their vocabulary. They may be angry and frustrated with the church. They may be wary of Christians. But for the most part, they are warm and welcoming and are usually quite normal. One of the most well-known Wiccans in the United States is a person you likely hear on the radio every day.

So Wiccan belief does not encompass good and evil; rather, the highest goal of a Wiccan is living a balanced life. Most Wiccans do follow an ethic they call the Wiccan Rede: "If it harms none, do what you will." They also believe in something called the Threefold Law: Anything you do will come back to you three times.

Seeking the Supernatural

Common to Wicca is the practice of magic and the casting of spells—symbolic acts performed in an altered state of consciousness in order to cause a desired change. Do Wiccans believe that magic really works? Yes. Every witch I spoke to had experienced the supernatural in some way. The witch activist named Starhawk defines *magic* as "the art of changing the consciousness of will."[5] When I heard her speak to a group of college students in California, she explained what that meant: "For instance, when you make a love spell, you have to think of what kind of love you want—woods in the moonlight love or the kind of love that says I will go pick up the kids after a soccer game type of love. You meditate on that kind of love and that sets things in motion."[6]

There are spells to overcome loneliness, to attract money, to bring inner power, to bind an enemy, and so on. Witches acknowledge that spells can be used for good or ill. Certainly there are stories about people who dabbled in witchcraft and inflicted harm on others. The Wiccans I met, however, did not become Wiccan to inflict harm. Most chose it because of dissatisfaction with the church and organized religion, a desire to have a real spiritual experience, or for political and social reasons.

A member of the Covenant of the Goddess told me during an interview at his home in Berkeley, California, that a wrong step when casting spells or connecting to a deity could bode ill for an underaged and inexperienced practitioner. He also said that older neo-Pagans fear lawsuits from parents if they teach interested young people how to practice magic.

Many Wiccans I met had experienced frightening episodes or knew of other Wiccans who had. Often, the spiritual reality of these episodes was exciting enough to persuade them to continue practicing the Craft, no matter how frightening the experience was.

Most Wiccans maintain a belief in the ability to communicate with the unseen spirit world, the occult. This includes psychic ability, clairvoyance, psychokinesis, and spirit communication. Then there is divination.

In her book *Witch Crafting: A Spiritual Guide to Making Magic*, Phyllis Curott instructs readers in "scrying," the practice of gazing at a mirror or other shiny object until a vision appears. "Scrying" is from the word *descry*, meaning "to make out dimly" or "to reveal."[7] She also describes Wicca as an amalgamation of free-masonry, mythology, folk practices, nineteenth-century American pantheism, transcendentalism, feminism, spiritualism, Buddhism, and shamanism.[8]

What Wiccans Agree On

Despite Wicca's lack of orthodoxy, there are a few tenets, rituals, and symbols that the majority of Wiccans would recognize. Most practitioners worship, experience, or invoke the Mother Goddess. They call her male consort the Horned God. Both are believed to be immanent deities who manifest themselves in nature. For instance, the moon, with its monthly cycle of waxing and waning, is perceived to be female and is considered a symbol of the Mother Goddess. The earth itself is also a symbol of the Mother Goddess because it gives forth fruit, vegetation, and life that sustain and nurture us. The sun, on the other hand, is male.

Sometimes the Goddess is represented by specific deities such as Artemis, the ancient Greek goddess of the hunt, or Gaia, goddess of the earth. Some Wiccans even claim that the Goddess is represented by Mary, the mother of Christ. Any strong woman or notable female in history can be dubbed "the Goddess."

The Horned God is often represented by ancient gods, such as the Greek mythological figure Pan, the Egyptian god Osiris, or the Norse god Thor. Most witches believe the Horned God dies and is reborn each year.

Wiccans typically celebrate eight *sabbats* centered on the solar cycles and twelve or thirteen *esbats* centered on the lunar cycles. These celebrations are thought to be times of heightened interaction between the natural and supernatural worlds. Many Wiccans today have adopted the Celtic calendar or "wheel of the year" and celebrate the seasonal pagan holidays of the British Isles during the pre-Christian period. These sabbat holidays* include Yule or winter solstice (around December 22), Imbolc (February 1 or 2), Ostara or spring equinox (March 21), Beltane (April 30), Mid-

---

* The exact dates of solstices and equinoxes vary from year to year.

summer or summer solstice (June 21), Lughnasadh (August 1), Mabon or autumn equinox (September 21), and Samhain (October 31).[9]

The Wiccan symbol is the pentagram, a five-pointed star representing air, fire, water, earth, and spirit. The tip of the pentagram always points upward, say Wiccans, because a pentagram pointing down represents Satanism.

THE NEW SALEM

As I spoke with the young woman who performed the spell casting in Salem, another walked up behind us. She introduced herself as Marisa, one of the primary visionaries of the Witch Village tour.

"This is all my creation," she said pointing to the elaborate set used for the spell casting. "We have spent months building stage sets and getting organized for this busy month."

Marisa told me she was one of the founding members of an organization that, according to the orange leaflet she handed me, seeks to educate visitors to the Witch City about who and what witches are and how they practice their faith in modern times. They educate visitors—Wiccan, Pagan, and non-Pagan—through open circles, public ritual, workshops, and guest lectures.

I met Marisa on my visit to Salem in October 2001 when America was still reeling from the terrorist attacks of September 11. Many Americans found comfort in moral absolutes following this event and saw the attacks as evidence that evil exists in the world. American flags flew on every available flagpole, and numerous cars sported We Support Our Troops bumper stickers.

Marisa disagreed. She rejected the notion of moral absolutes. Americans had no right to condemn Osama bin Laden for his worldview, she told me. Instead, she proposed redirecting energy to create more harmony and balance in the universe. Men and women are supposed to be equal, she explained. Things got out of balance because the Taliban persecuted women. The natural order of things was upset and needed to be righted. Because Wiccans believe in karma and the Threefold Law, they believe that Bin Laden will get his punishment eventually, and we should throw good energy his way in the meantime. At times it *is* necessary to take action, Pagans believe, and they are active at protesting certain things. But I found that many remain inconsistent in how they determine when action is appropriate and when it is not.

By day Marisa works as a professional tattoo artist. It was her Italian grandmother who introduced her to witchcraft as a child. Both of her parents are witches and were initiated into the coven of Laurie Cabot, who was dubbed in the mid-1970s by then-governor of Massachusetts, Michael Dukakis, the "official witch" of Salem.[10] Marisa's parents now practice their own eclectic version of witchcraft, while Marisa practices Welsh witchcraft and has also been initiated into the Gardnerian tradition, which we'll learn more about later.

From the Witch Village, I wandered into a shop called Artemesia Botanicals, which calls itself Salem's Herbal Apothecary. The aroma of sweet-smelling oils and herbs greeted me as I entered. The shop clerk was in a good mood because she was looking forward to the annual Feast of Samhain that night.

The witches I encountered in Salem celebrated the ancient pagan Celtic holidays, such as Samhain. Samhain honors ancestors and serves as the New Year for modern witches. The ancient Celts and modern witches believe that "the veil" between the living and the dead is thin at Samhain, according to Salem's Witches Education Bureau. Wiccans believe that during this time the spirits of the dead are able to cross over into the land of the living and be with their loved ones.

Preregistered guests had been dropping by Artemesia Botanicals all day to pick up their tickets for the evening feast. The shop served as the registration site for all the witchcraft-related events in October. Earlier in the month, tickets had been available for an event called Ask a Witch—Make a Wand, where witches answered questions from the public about modern witchcraft.

As I left Artemesia Botanicals, I saw a group of women wearing purple and black capes gathering outside another shop. A line snaked its way around the building. As I approached, I saw that it was another metaphysical shop. Cautiously I joined the line and soon entered the dimly lighted shop. The shop was small and crowded, and I inched my way along the wall of merchandise. Ritual daggers with jeweled handles lay in locked glass display cabinets next to amethyst-encrusted chalices and silver goblets. On the far wall was an assortment of pentagrams and clay goddesses. I even spied goddess-shaped soap. As I left the shop, I noticed a rack of bumper stickers for sale. Pagan and Proud read one. Another read W.A.S.P., White Anglo-Saxon Pagan, which accurately described the lack of ethnic diversity among the neo-Pagans I encountered in Massachusetts. Another simply read Blessed Be!

Around the corner Laurie Cabot held court; a line turned out the door of a shop where she was selling and signing her latest book. I had read an article about Cabot in which she told the reporter that Wicca is "pre-Christian, an Earth religion. There are two supremes, a god and a goddess. It's an art, a science and a religion." Cabot uses spells and charms "to bring about health, happiness and prosperity for people, animals and plants."[11]

Over the years Cabot has been criticized by fellow witches for commercializing the Craft. A Californian, she left her life as a showgirl and enjoys her high-profile role as a witch. She is even listed in the Salem Chamber of Commerce directory under "witches." Cabot became a witch at sixteen and claims to have a coven in Salem with more than two thousand members.[12] A Salem witch told me that Cabot has made it possible for those who desire to walk the streets in a robe and pentagram to feel perfectly safe, a far cry from the Salem of yesterday.

GROWING POPULARITY

"Many witches flock to Salem on Halloween because they know there will be other witches they can meet here," a woman with long blond hair and a white cape told me outside the Witch Village tour. A self-described witch, she had traveled to Salem to speak to tourists on behalf of real witches as part of her coven's education outreach effort. She and a group of witches stood under a tent that had been erected next to the Witch Village warehouse. As we spoke, screams and stage smoke emanated from the Haunted House as hordes of teenagers wandered in and out.

"Wicca has become incredibly popular in the past ten years. It used to be that only a witch could make a witch—you had to serve for a year and a day. Now witches can self-initiate or self-dedicate." Kids, she said, are not as interested in learning the strict coven structures. They find information about witchcraft online and teach themselves. She said she always knew that she was a witch because her family recycled, created compost, and grew and ate vegetables from their land for many years, long before it was popular.

This behavior, however, would seem at most to have made them naturalists, and as she spoke, I found myself thinking back to my own childhood in Oxfordshire, England. We, too, recycled and grew vegetables and fruit. My mother, who is from North Carolina, made lots of homemade jams, apple jellies, and various chutneys from fruits and vegetables that grew on our property. No one in my family would have thought of this as avant-garde or trendsetting behavior. We used to pick blackberries in our own garden, and most nights my mother sent one of us to pull a head of lettuce out of the ground to make a salad for dinner. We added all the waste from the fruits and vegetables in our garden to the compost heap. I had never thought of us as witches! We were Anglicans who enjoyed gardening and the bounty that provided. But as I listened to the woman in Salem, I knew that because much of modern life has lost its connection to the land, people are desperate to rediscover that connection. Wicca, with its emphasis on nature and the change of seasons, is a popular way to spiritualize the longing to be reconnected to the earth.

As we talked, a man walked up to join our conversation. He was dressed in a black shirt and jeans and wore a dark green cloak.

"I am a witch," he announced. He told me he lived in Connecticut where he worked as an engineer, but he came to Salem to visit with other witches. "I had a recent tragedy in my life, and I wanted to connect with people. These people just gave me a hug and made me feel at home."

Not So Strange

As night fell upon Salem, the streets became thick with trick-or-treaters and other moonlight revelers. I saw Marisa make her way through the crowd downtown. She was preparing for the torchlight procession that would weave its way through Salem that night. The procession was to culminate in a ritual circle. She handed me an orange flier that described the event.

"Here you go. Hope you come!"

I looked at the piece of paper. Drawn around the announcement were skulls, the sun, the moon, pentagrams, and half-naked women carrying torches of fire.

"Spirit of Samhain!" it read. "Torchlight Procession and Fifth Annual Sabbat Circle. Please bring a candle or torch, drums, rattles, and bells. Magickal-themed costumes and Witch finery are highly encouraged! We will be parading through Salem to Mack Park—where Samhain fire should burn in accordance with ancient tradition!"

As Marisa hurried away, I tucked the flier into my pocket. I had decided to instead attend another Samhain ritual being held on Gallows Hill, the site of the hangings in Salem Village. As I trekked up to Gallows Hill on the outskirts of town, I thought of the women who had walked this path before me. One of them, Susannah Martin, stood accused of "Sundry acts of Witchcraft." "She defiantly laughed at her accusers, one of whom fell into a fit during the trial."

" 'Well I may [laugh] at such folly,' Martin told her inquisitors, according to court records. 'I have no hand in witchcraft.' Ten days later, Martin was hanged."[13]

But the crowded scene on Gallows Hill that I witnessed that night was very different from what it must have been like more than three hundred years ago at the height of the witch trials in Salem. The night air was crisp as hundreds of men and women gathered, set up the altar, hugged, and greeted one another. No one was denying the practice of witchcraft. They embraced it. The one hundred or so spectators were told to stand back. We stood silently in concentric circles around the group of witches in the middle.

"Hear us, O great Goddess! Diana! Astarte! Brigid! Thou Great Mother whom we adore, grant us our passions," shouted a woman from the center of the circle as she called on the names of ancient pagan goddesses. Diana is the Roman goddess of wild animals and the hunt; Astarte is an ancient Canaanite fertility goddess; and Brigid is the Celtic goddess of smithcraft and healing. The entire group began to chant in lilting rhythms, "Earth I am, Spirit I am, Air and Fire and Water I am!"

The voices of four hundred witches filled the night air. I stood next to an archway made of wire that was stuffed with autumn leaves. At its feet were two jack-o'-lanterns burning brightly. Incense filled the air. Soon the witches called on everyone present to link arms and pass beneath the arbor of autumn leaves. The circle started to move swiftly as the witches kept a regular beat on their drums.

After everyone had passed beneath the arbor, a man clad in black with a crown of antlers on his head ran around the circle carrying a sword, creating what he called sacred space, a common Wiccan ritual performed to prevent unwanted spirits from entering during the magic.

A film crew from the Discovery Channel sat quietly in the shadows behind me, making a documentary on the growth of Wicca in the United States. The spectacle seemed bizarre to the camera crew.

"We have been gathering film and information for a while about the Wiccan religion," one cameraman whispered to me, "but this is the strangest thing we have ever seen."

As I would continue to find out, it is not so unusual anymore.

Tired of Sitting in Pews

Why Wicca?

Once a month, in an old ballroom in downtown Oakland, California, hundreds of people from age five to seventy-five gather to celebrate mass. Presiding over each evening is Episcopal priest Matthew Fox. His Saint Patrick's Day mass, called the Techno Cosmic Mass, bore little resemblance to the sacrament of the Lord's Supper that I had grown up with in the Anglican Church. Instead, it was a mix of Paganism, witchcraft, nature worship, drama, art, dance, and a multimedia presentation.

The mass was attended by ordinary people—families with strollers and complicated lives, seeking spiritual answers, as we all are. Celtic music played as we entered the dark, cavernous ballroom. Six large video screens were situated around the room. Altars featured Christian and pagan images.

Fox began the ceremony: "We are tired of being preached at in pews," he bellowed from the raised platform. Everyone cheered. "We like to be able to participate, and that is what you will do tonight!"[1] Whooping and hollering filled the room as he sat down.

The room was then plunged into darkness, except for the flickering images on the television screens. All eyes were transfixed on the altar in the center of the room. Slowly a small Hispanic woman with long black hair approached the altar holding an *athame*—a ceremonial dagger used by witches in their rituals—and performed a Wiccan ritual known as "calling the directions." Walking rapidly around the altar with the knife between her hands, she intended to harness energy as the evening began.

After a short talk from another woman and a time of dancing and lament, a procession of ten people wearing masks approached the central altar carrying the communion bread and wine. Fox, who calls himself a panentheist,* began the communion ceremony. He prayed to the Great Spirit. Rather than invoking Christ's body and blood as an atoning sacrifice for sin, he invoked the name of Christ as a good example of someone whose life of compassion is one we ought to mirror. Indeed, I noticed that the message that Christ conveyed during his Last Supper was entirely absent.

Fox's listeners sat on the floor wide-eyed. His disregard for the deeply held beliefs of so many Christians around the world was startling to me because he was attempting to reach out to others in the name of Christ. The atmosphere began to feel oppressive. The people who were presenting the bread and wine continued to wear their masks as Fox invoked Christ and the Great Spirit. As I stared at the masks, a frightening sense of darkness and heaviness began to descend on me. I knew I had to get out. I turned and ran out of the room.

What I witnessed seemed to be a perversion of the simple meal during which Christ shared the message of his atoning sacrifice and washed the feet of those present. I felt heartbroken because I had seen a group of people desperate to find meaning in life, desperate to have a voice in their religious practice, being given the wrong message about who Jesus is. If anyone had come seeking the truth of the gospel, he or she would not have found it.

The cheer that had erupted when Fox announced that they were tired

---

* Panentheism should not be confused with pantheism. Panentheism acknowledges that the Divine is not equal to the earth, but all things exist in the Divine.

of sitting in pews rang in my ears as I walked to my car. The church should be a place where such creative people thrive! But the palpable angst and frustration in that room reminded me that often it is not. The people attending the ceremony that night were searching for truth and a real spirituality. Many had long ago abandoned all hope of finding that within Christendom and were looking instead to Wicca for answers.

LOOKING FOR ALTERNATIVES

Why do hundreds of thousands of Americans embrace Wicca? Why do they believe that Christianity has failed them? In my research I uncovered manifold personal reasons why seekers had a foot out the door of the church and were turning to Wicca. Here are just a few:

1. *Concern for the earth.* One common reason for leaving the church was a love of nature. Wiccans love the earth and care deeply for the environment, and they feel that the American church has largely been silent when it comes to stewardship of creation. How many sermons are preached on caring for the environment, being good stewards, and preserving what we have for future generations?

2. *Empowerment for women.* Another reason Americans are embracing Wicca is that women have been wounded by the church. They have been treated as second-class citizens for too much of Christian history. Many Wiccan women told me that their gifts had been confined to teaching Sunday school and making coffee, when they wanted to do so much more for the kingdom of God.

3. *Frustration with the consumer culture.* Wiccans who have left the Christian church also told me they were turned off by the consumer culture that has gripped modern evangelicalism as well as the political stran-

glehold the so-called Christian Right appears to have on evangelicals. They were frustrated that the effects of globalization on the working poor in the United States and abroad are not as much of a concern in some churches as individual piety, important as that is.

4. The draw of the supernatural. Other Wiccans told me they were looking for a spirituality that is real. Pollster George Gallup reports that Americans are spiritually hungry and have an intense desire for religious and spiritual growth. But Gallup and coauthor Michael Lindsay also found that the key factor for a person going to church is feeling "that a supernatural transition is going on, lives are being changed, and people are excited about their faith."[2] Spiritual seekers know they are missing something. They not only want to know things intellectually; they also want to supernaturally sense spiritual truth.

The irony is that often the last people to believe in the supernatural today are the men and women in mainline Christian churches, who are, as Os Guinness wrote more than thirty years ago in his salient book *The Dust of Death,* "lulled complacently to sleep by the smug rationalism of their theology."[3] Wiccans and orthodox Christians may both agree that the supernatural exists, but I learned from my conversations with Wiccans that, in their experience, many churches ignore the reality of an unseen world. Church becomes another boring social exercise, and in our busy lives, who has time for that? Churches that don't encourage all the "basics"—forgiveness of sins, a relationship with Christ, and the indwelling of the Holy Spirit—quickly lose people to alternative religions that *do* offer supernatural experiences.

We in the West have a lot to learn from our brothers and sisters in the developing world when it comes to the supernatural. Their world is far less cluttered than ours. They live closer to the earth; they know its cycles and rhythms. Indeed, they are often at its mercy and pray for miracles to occur. Because of this, they are more open to the supernatural.

I have a friend who lived in Cameroon for a year, and one thing that struck her when she moved to London was the abundance of fruit in the supermarket in the middle of winter. In Cameroon she had grown accustomed to waiting in anticipation for the seasons to change so the fruit that grew during a particular season would be available. She felt as if she awakened, like the earth, to bring forth fruit when it was ripe. The seasons themselves and the fruit that comes with them are cause to rejoice. They are miracles.

In the West we are completely removed from these rhythms of life. In London my friend was almost sorry that she could get ripe tomatoes in December. Our efficiency has removed much wonder from our lives and has erased the expectation of it. This is what Wiccans are trying to regain in so many instances. As alienation from the natural world continues, more and more people will seek supernatural and spiritual experiences.

HYPOCRISY IN THE CHURCH

The number-one reason I heard for leaving the church and turning to Wicca was perceived hypocrisy among Christians. Nowhere in my travels was this sentiment more pronounced among neo-Pagans than in southern states. This was of particular interest to me because of my own southern heritage. Churches flourish on many a street corner in southern towns. Some people attend church because they have found ultimate peace and truth in the message of Jesus Christ. Others attend for social reasons, to project the ideal of an upstanding citizen.

But an astute seeker searching for a spirituality that is real soon sees through the facade of social Christianity. Faith that is not real gets replaced with something that is real. And in many cases, Wicca's emphasis on magic and altered consciousness fits the bill.

One of the people I met who had turned from the church to Wicca was a woman we'll call Ginny, who is the high priestess of a pagan advocacy group in the mountains of North Carolina. The group has between one and two hundred members and celebrates pagan holidays together. Members are politically active. They also organize events for their children, including a Vacation Witchcraft School that is listed in the newspaper alongside the Vacation Bible Schools.

Ginny and her advocacy group particularly feel animosity toward the local Christian community, which reveals a lack of harmony and tolerance in Pagan circles as well. Ginny told me she thought of Christians as shallow and unwilling to understand her family's religious practices. "My daughter has had a terrible time at school," she explained, describing to me the taunts and jeers that her elementary school–age child had experienced.

I asked Ginny if she is generally hostile to Christians. It seemed as if she was demonizing them in a way that she would not like to have been treated herself.

"I *have* been accused of being anti-Christian," she replied cagily. "I mean in activism work, they *are* kind of the enemy."

Ginny and I met at a Dairy Queen on the outskirts of Asheville, North Carolina. She was a consummate example of witchcraft going mainstream. She explained to me that Dianic witches "are feminists and left-wing ladies, often lesbians, but not always. We have some covens that preach ritual sex, drug use, and polygamy. The way they worship the Goddess is through sex. The way they worship nature is through mushrooms and pot!"

Ginny's candor was refreshing after I had pored over so much academic jargon about Wicca. She insisted that not all Pagans are polygamists and smoke pot, but I appreciated that she was as forthright about the intricacies of neo-Paganism as her outfit was about her physical condition—a bright pink and blue shirt with a stork on the front indicated that she was pregnant.

"I am technically a witch," she told me when I asked her about her religious background. "I am not Wiccan—which is a particular tradition from England. I call myself a traditional family witch. I worship eight deities, four gods and four goddesses, and do a lot of practical folk magic rather than the ceremonial or ritual magic of the Wiccans."

I asked her if she would consider herself a Wiccan at all, and she vehemently told me that she did not. I leaned forward, intrigued by her answer.

"Wicca is a very recent development invented in the mid-twentieth century by men—Gerald Gardner and Aleister Crowley, among others. Gardner and Crowley were interested in the drug culture and free love. They had a lot of ritual sex, which is not appealing to me but appeals to rebellious teenagers who would do anything to freak out their parents."

As a witch, Ginny takes an unusual position in the Pagan community on abortion. She is pro-life.

"For me, it's all about respect for nature," she said. "Human life is part of nature. My views are out of the mainstream among witches. Most favor abortion on demand, which I view as essentially selfish." She told me, in fact, that many teens like Wicca because it indulges their selfish side and does not ask much of them. Ginny also confessed that there was often a great deal of infighting within the Pagan community, just as there is in the Christian church. Pagans accuse the Christian church of infighting and yet they have to deal with it in their own group as well, which reveals, more than anything, our fallen human nature.

She paused to take a sip of her drink. Her cell phone rang. It was her husband calling from home where he was taking care of their five kids. The sixth, on the way, would be her last, she told me.

As I left the Dairy Queen, I realized that Ginny was one of the first witches I had met who made me realize how ordinary they could be. She was politically active against Christians but would never wish them any harm. She just wanted more Pagans to speak out about what they believed and not be intimidated. Sadly, many Christians don't take the time to get to know people like Ginny; instead, they judge her from afar. And, like Ginny, many Pagans judge Christians from afar. This only further alienates neo-Pagans from Christians. It would be better if Christians defied the stereotypes by getting to know neo-Pagans, as the apostle Paul did.

At a Beltane festival outside Charlottesville, Virginia, I met Laura, a witch in her mid-twenties who had a small son and a husband in the U.S. Navy. Laura seemed to feel the same way about Christians as Ginny did. Brimming with excitement, she walked breathless into the tent where I was sitting with another Wiccan named Donna. Laura started talking animatedly about certain rituals she had been helping organize at the festival. She admitted that as a witch she sometimes felt discriminated against for her beliefs. We agreed that many people of sincere faith who are trying to make a difference in society can be maligned for their efforts.

Laura's demeanor darkened when the discussion turned to Christians. "There has been hundreds of years of bad publicity from Christians," she said, referring to her dislike of the church and of Christians who have given Christianity a bad name.

"But things would be a lot different if Christians actually acted like Christ. We'd all be a lot better off," noted Donna.

"People need so badly for something to believe in," Laura said rather philosophically. "Monsters live inside of everybody, and we have to tame them somehow. I choose a Pagan path to do this."

Another witch at the Beltane festival called herself a "lapsed Methodist." Petra lived in Lynchburg, Virginia, and had pagan bumper stickers on her car. She was often followed closely by other cars, and some people even followed her into the grocery store, pointing and staring at her from a distance. This unnerved her. She assumed these people were Christians because she lived in Lynchburg, which is, she added pointedly, "the home of Jerry Falwell." Regardless of whether they were actually Christians, I assured her that I would not behave that way toward people at the festival. She gave me a hug and told me she was glad that I would listen to what people had to say.

"And, you know, if Jesus were here, he would most likely sit among us and at least listen to us!" She laughed cheerily. Jesus. She and Donna had brought him up without my even asking about him. No one had a bad word to say about him during my research. Ever. Talking about Jesus is always a great conversation starter with neo-Pagans.

FLEEING THE EXTREMES

While I was researching this book, a troubling article appeared in the *Los Angeles Times* about an incident that captures many of the tensions between Wiccans and Christians. A group of Wiccans in Orange County had gotten up early to welcome the sunrise with a ritual on Midsummer's Day. They had set up their ceremony in an empty parking lot, and events were underway when a group of no doubt well-intentioned Christians came and surrounded them with their cars. One blasted loud Christian rock music out of his SUV stereo and called on the Wiccans to repent. As a Christian,

I read this and sighed. The very fact that the Christians were driving gas-guzzling, earth-*unfriendly* SUVs would have been the first turnoff to these earth-worshiping people. And it is simply rude to blare loud rock music at anyone early in the morning, no matter what the lyrics. This incident came to be known locally as "Wiccagate."

The sad reality is that people who are drawn to Wicca, who love nature and believe in justice for women, are not likely to hear these issues discussed by Christians typically portrayed in the popular media. This SUV-driving group did nothing to alter the stereotype either. After the Christians' behavior in Orange County, Wiccans certainly aren't going to want to darken the doors of a church! Unfortunately, the media tends to ignore the good work and deeds of the Christians who care about the same issues Wiccans do.

So Wiccans flee from two stereotypical extremes: the Christian churches that rationally deny the supernatural, and the evangelicals who act like those in Orange County.

A MIXED BAG

The irony is that modern Pagans and Wiccans still borrow heavily from Judeo-Christian values. By being essentially pantheists and monists, they have little basis on which to condemn anything. Charles Manson was at least honest when he asked, "If God is one, what is bad?"[4] Still, neo-Pagans believe in sin without naming it as such, for they feel indignant over social injustice, mistreatment of the environment, and the hypocrisy of the church. They believe that men and women commit wrongs that must be righted. But many Wiccans don't want to take on the guilt those standards might bring to their own lives, except in some areas of their lives in which they feel comfortable making a change.

The greatest way to make a difference in the world is to apply a universal truth of what is right and wrong not only to others but to yourself. The first person to start with is the person in the mirror. This is the message of the gospel. But the gospel message has been obscured in Western culture.

Jonathan Rauch in the *Atlantic Monthly* writes, "The greatest development in modern religion is not a religion at all—it's an attitude best described as 'apatheism.'"[5] *Apatheism* is not agnosticism or atheism but a combination of the two words *apathetic* and *theism*. Apatheism summarizes well the religious state of many Americans today—and highlights how Wiccans are different. Most Wiccans have thought more seriously about spirituality and some of life's big questions than many in the secular and even Christian cultures. They have not been content to skate through life seeking the gods of fashion, peer pressure, or materialism, reserving religion for weekends and special holidays.

Think of your typical college student today. She is bright and articulate. She was raised in postfeminist America. She is very aware of injustice toward women worldwide. She is horrified by the corruption within a prominent face of Christianity—the Roman Catholic Church. She also knows that our planet's resources are finite. A religion that claims to promote women and respect for the earth and that emphasizes our spiritual nature would be greatly appealing. Wicca claims to offer all of these elements. The question this student might ask is, "Why *not* Wicca?" Cultural forces, the media, entertainment, and the Internet have certainly provided her easy access to Wicca and neo-Paganism. For, as we will see in the next chapter, cultural forces have shaped the practice of Wicca whether practitioners like it or not.

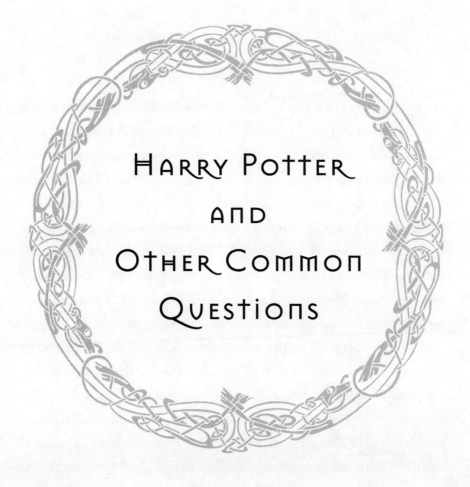

HARRY POTTER AND OTHER COMMON QUESTIONS

Why Now?

Are the Harry Potter books the reason why Wicca has become more mainstream? Judging from the number of times I have been asked that question, I wouldn't be surprised if some readers turned right to this chapter! My quick answer is that the popular Harry Potter series has little to do with Wicca. But it is true that although it used to be hard to find Wiccan books and paraphernalia—such as wands, herbs, candles, knives, and capes—that is no longer the case. The 1990s lessened the inhibitions young people used to have about entering occult stores, and now Wiccan items and books are carried in the larger chains in brightly lighted suburban malls and shopping centers. Why has this happened?

Based on the trends in American society as a whole, the time is ripe for Wicca to take root. As David Rieff wrote in *Harper's* magazine, multiculturalism is good for business. Rieff pointed out that the Afrocentric holiday, Kwanzaa, is a moneymaker for retailers who manufacture and sell Kwanzaa items.[1] The same is true for Wicca, which has become subject to America's almighty dollar. Advertising executives love to find niche markets. They've commercialized a formerly marginal spirituality into full-blown Wicca chic. Enter almost any bookstore in America, and you will find books—sometimes scores of them—on Wicca, Paganism, Goddess worship, and women's spirituality. If you watch carefully while driving on the highway, you'll see bumper stickers that read The Goddess Is Alive, Magic Is Afoot! Log on to the Internet and type the word *witch* or *Wicca* into a search engine, and thousands of Web-site listings appear. And Hollywood has cashed in on the interest for years with TV programs such as *Buffy the Vampire Slayer* and *Charmed* and films such as *Practical Magic* and *The Craft*.

In this chapter we'll look at all three phenomena: Harry Potter and the publishing industry, the effects of the Internet, and the influence of popular TV programs and movies.

Harry Potter's Influence

London-based Bloomsbury Publishing published the first Harry Potter book in 1997, and Scholastic Books published the Potter series in America in 1998. The series is based on the life of a young wizard named Harry Potter whose parents are killed shortly after his birth by the evil Lord Voldemort. Through a bizarre series of events, Harry finds himself at Hogwarts School for Witchcraft and Wizardry where he and his friends have many adventures. Each book charts a year of Harry's progress through the school. The books have sold millions of copies worldwide for author J. K. Rowling, have been made into a series of major motion pictures, and have won several awards.

Unlike Wicca, Rowling's books actually promote a clear understanding of good and evil. There are no gods and goddesses to worship and no pantheistic teaching that all is one and humans are divine. The stories and themes that fill the pages of the Harry Potter books have little to do with Wicca at all, in fact.

The books do glorify magic and make fun of ordinary humans known to Harry and his friends as "muggles." This should come as no surprise since children relish stories about other children using magic to make fun of adults. Children have always been fascinated by magic, as are most adults. For parents with Christian convictions, questions as to what they should or shouldn't allow their children to read or watch are very serious. Author Connie Neal has written one thoughtful book about the Harry Potter phenomenon to help Christian parents decide whether to let their children read the series. (See the resources section in the back of this book for more information.)

The vice president of Minneapolis-based New Age and metaphysical publisher Llewellyn noted in an interview with *Publishers Weekly* that the surge of interest in Wicca is part of the Harry Potter phenomenon and has created a larger number of readers and practitioners. "The younger audience keeps eating that kind of stuff up," he said.[2] I agree with him that although the Harry Potter series is not about Wicca per se, it has helped open doors to Wiccan books and trends. In conversations with teenagers, I have found that although some of them read the Harry Potter books as preteens and then migrated to serious books based on Wicca as they grew older, many simply read Harry Potter when they read The Lord of the Rings or *The Lion, the Witch and the Wardrobe*.

I was surprised to learn that publishers of Wicca books have fielded few complaints about their books or spell kits from alarmed parents or concerned Christians, while many Christian parents have complained that J. K. Rowling is teaching their children to become witches. As we will see, although Harry Potter has little to do with Wicca, its popularity has obviously encouraged publishers to release more books based explicitly on neo-Paganism.

Novels Based on Wicca

While Harry Potter is a fictional series about British schoolchildren attending magic school, the Wicca books that have multiplied as a result of the Harry Potter popularity are about a very real practice. Access to these books has enabled young people to practice witchcraft with their very own pagan altars in their own bedrooms.

After witnessing the Harry Potter craze, publishing houses began paperback-fiction series centered on teenage girls' involvement in witchcraft. And what child does not wish she had magic powers? Penguin Putnam published a series titled Sweep by Cate Tiernan. Under its Volo imprint, Hyperion published the Daughters of the Moon series by Lynne Ewing. And Avon Books published a series titled Circle of Three by Isobel Bird. Scholastic, which publishes the Harry Potter books, hopes to capitalize on their success with a series aimed at preteens titled T*Witches. With standard plot lines and stock characters, all of the books rely on the typical teenage themes of love and peer pressure, dressed up in witchcraft to give them an exotic edge.

The first book in the Sweep series was called the *Book of Shadows*—the title borrowed from Gerald Gardner's first Wiccan spell book—and was advertised in *Seventeen* magazine with the banner headline "Life, Love, Witchcraft: Sweep: A Hot New Series That Will Leave You Spellbound!"

The books contain Cinderella-type stories about a Catholic schoolgirl named Morgan. Morgan is in love with a classmate named Cal, who is a practicing Wiccan and is embarrassed that Morgan is a virgin. Cal throws a party and invites Morgan, who joins in the activities of his coven, dances in a circle, and chants "blessed be" and thanks to the "goddess" and "god."

Morgan feels invigorated after the ritual, starts shopping at the local occult bookstore, finds new witch friends, and is transformed from a shy girl into a beautiful young woman with supernatural powers. She rejects her Catholicism and begins to hide ritual tools in her bedroom.

By the fourth book, however, Cal turns out to be the "evil witch" who tried to burn Morgan alive, which is interesting in light of the fact that he tells Morgan that Wicca is tame and inclusive. Morgan dumps Cal but continues to participate in her coven.

Author Cate Tiernan is not a witch, saying that even Wicca is "too organized" for her.[3] Tiernan's books resonate with impressionable young readers, however, as evidenced by dialogue on a Web site devoted to the Sweep books that is maintained by a young fan.

The other series are similar to the Sweep series. T*Witches is about twin witches, and Daughters of the Moon is about teenage girls who have magical powers and become goddesses.

The Volo imprint has also published a series of books called W.I.T.C.H., marketed to the four- to eight-year-old group. W.I.T.C.H. stands for five friends, Will, Irma, Taranee, Cornelia, and Hay Lin, each of whom has the power to control a natural element—air, water, fire, earth, and something called the mysterious Heart of Candracar. Wiccans would also hope to control the natural elements in their spells.

Hyperion's representative told me they wanted to do a fantasy for girls about girl power and knew it would sell well based on sales of other books in that genre.

Wicca the Moneymaker

The major bookstore chains know that Wicca is a moneymaker and have stocked their shelves accordingly. Most of the books are of the how-to variety—how to build an altar, cast a spell, pray to the Goddess, and so forth—with some of the previously mentioned fiction series beginning to appear for teens.

"Wicca is a steady category for us," a representative from the headquarters of a large bookstore chain told me. "It seems like there is actually a flood of books on the market, perhaps because of the Internet, which has publicized Wicca in a way it has never been before." Recognizing a hot market, this bookseller now publishes Wicca titles under its imprint.

One book, has an eye-catching pink and purple cover and is filled with love spells and prosperity spells. While most Wiccans roll their eyes at books like this, many confess to owning a few, and some admit that such books introduced them to Wicca.

Another large bookstore chain experienced an increased interest in books about Wicca in the 1990s, a trend that has continued. After the terrorist attacks of September 11, sales of spiritual books went up, and Wicca book sales remained steady. This popular bookseller reports an increased interest in Wicca among teenagers, which their buyer attributes to the proliferation of information about Wicca on the Internet, as well as TV programs such as *Charmed*. The Wicca books that sell the best for this bookstore chain are those devoted to love spells or prosperity spells.

There is even *The Complete Idiot's Guide to Wicca and Witchcraft*, published by Alpha Books, for the unintelligent, uninitiated, or intimidated-but-curious reader. "This is a good line for us," Alpha's acquisitions editor told me. "We decided to do it because there was so much about witchcraft in the media, with shows like *Buffy the Vampire Slayer* and *Sabrina the Teenage Witch*. We did a lot of research. Many of our readers are women, and this appeals to them." The author of the *Idiot's Guide* is a practicing Wiccan who owns her own shop in Baltimore. The book is one of Alpha's bestsellers.

ECW (Essays on Canadian Writing), a Canadian publishing house that got its start by publishing academic essays, leaped into the Wicca market in 2000 with two books about Wicca: *Magickal Weddings* by Joy Ferguson and *Witchcraft and the Web* by M. Macha Nightmare, an elder and minister in the Covenant of the Goddess. But the books don't sell as well in Canada.

"Our big market is the States," ECW's publicist said. "There are so many Pagan gatherings where we can promote our books. There are twenty-five-hundred people alone who attend the Heartland Pagan Festival in Kansas City every spring. That is pretty astonishing." ECW's promotional material touts the role the Internet has played in spreading Wicca throughout the United States.

Llewellyn has also capitalized on the popular interest in Wicca. After more than one hundred years of publishing books, Llewellyn has entered mainstream bookshops rather than selling its books only in small metaphysical shops. In 1996 Llewellyn noticed a surge in sales with the release of *The Craft,* a movie about a small coven of teenage witches. In 1999, when the publisher's title *Teen Witch: Wicca for a New Generation* came out, a publicist at Llewellyn told me the book sold more copies by year's end than any other book Llewellyn had published in its ninety-five-year history. Many teens credit this book for introducing them to Wicca. The book lists countless spells, such as the "elf locker spell," which keeps classmates from breaking into your locker, or the "crabby teacher spell," which is meant to sweeten the disposition of unpopular teachers.

The author of *Teen Witch,* a Wiccan high priestess named Silver RavenWolf, writes an introduction to her book for parents whose children are interested in Wicca and may have bought her book out of curiosity. RavenWolf acknowledges that Wicca has dangerous aspects but goes on to assure parents that her book will show their children how to avoid the "bad places." Later in the book she attacks parental authority in the home, however, and scolds parents for telling their children what religion is and is not.

In addition to books, Silver RavenWolf sells "teen witch kits" that retail for $24.95. *Publishers Weekly* reported sales of twenty-four-thousand kits after six months on the shelf. The kit comes complete with a crystal, a pentagram necklace, a spell book, spell salt, and a pop-up altar.

Responding to the Culture

Publishers troll the Internet to find the latest trends in Wicca and gain insight into the needs of the Pagan community. One evident trend, *Publishers Weekly* reported, is that teens are no longer interested in conventional religion. The magazine trumpeted this finding in an article titled "Nurturing Today's Teen Spirit" with the subheading "Authentic and extreme—with strong graphics—are in; preachy and bland are out." Teens are interested in religion and spirituality with a twist. "Teen Bibles, teen books about Wicca and other books about spirituality written just for adolescents are going strong," notes the article.[4] All the publishers interviewed for the article feared that teens are not interested in dogma, apologetics, and theology but rather are interested in more practical books about how to live out their faith in their daily lives. In Llewellyn's *Wild Girls: The Path of the Young Goddess,* for instance, author Patricia Monaghan tells the stories of goddesses in the folklore of different countries and teaches teen readers to make crafty objects, such as meditation pillows.

An associate editor at Penguin Putnam told me that her company is marketing a set of books about Wicca in hopes of reaching a broad audience: "We do feel that in order to have a wide appeal, a book for teens on the subject [Wicca] would have to take a darker, more sophisticated tone."

THE WICCAN WEB

To better understand the rapid growth of neo-Paganism, it is necessary to search neo-Pagan Web sites. More likely than not, you'll find that Wiccan activities have been occurring in your area for a long time. As I mentioned earlier, one of the reasons for the surge in popularity of neo-Pagan books and paraphernalia in the 1990s was the Internet. Many spiritual seekers find that the Internet offers a sense of community in our increasingly fragmented society. The Barna Research Group recently released a poll indicating that during this decade, fifty million Americans will seek to have their spiritual experience solely through the Internet, and upwards of one hundred million Americans will rely on the Internet to deliver some aspects of their religious experience.[5] The Internet has indeed opened up a new "virtual" world to the Pagan community that previously never existed. Today a witch in Salem can communicate with another in Duluth with a click of the mouse. Curious teens have a wealth of information at their fingertips. Through increased Internet sales of Wicca-related books and paraphernalia, a sort of pop-Paganism has been created. Parents who use the Internet exclusively for e-mail, basic research, and purchases will not encounter much of this, but young people who surf the Internet are bombarded with it daily.

In the past, someone turned off by Christianity would have become an agnostic or an atheist. A Catholic might have shocked his family by becoming a Protestant or vice versa, or someone might have converted to Judaism. But seekers did not have many other visible options. In the sixties things changed, but hardly anyone would have admitted to practicing witchcraft. The Internet and mass communication, however, have changed all that. We have more information today than ever before. Seekers now feel more comfortable embracing Wicca because of the Internet. They have a wealth of information about an unusual spiritual practice at their fingertips and discover that others are searching too. Those who would have been culturally marginalized in the past have an instant community. The Internet also allows anonymous interaction, which is appealing for those whose pagan practices might not be welcomed in their homes or schools.

An editor at New York's Citadel Press says it is no surprise that Wicca grew as the Internet did. "Wiccans organized themselves very well, and they are very Web oriented, which has allowed them to become more of a movement and make others aware of what they believe," he told me. "Our first book was called *The Modern Witch's Spellbook* by Sarah Morrison, thirty years ago. Then books about love spells became popular at the same time that the environmental movement took off, which was embraced by Wiccans as sort of a return to Mother Earth, the Mother Goddess."

Citadel even has a book titled *The Wiccan Web: Surfing the Magic on the Internet* by Patricia Telesco and Sirona Knight, which provides instruction to young witches for setting up their own computer altar, blessing and consecrating it, casting "techno spells," and performing "cyber-rituals."

Does Citadel see these books as serious?

"Oh no!" the editor laughed. "It is solely for entertainment purposes. We did make sure all of the materials used were approved as authentic, however, but we have no intention of anyone using it for anything but fun."

Market-savvy publishers like Citadel are catering to this market of online faith shoppers. *The Wiccan Web* is strictly a how-to book. Its contents range from chants and spells for diagnosing computer problems to a list of what the authors call "Wicca Speak emoticons," such as $# (representing a prosperity magic) or D——:-) (symbolizing a toast for the god and goddess). The authors have taken entire lists of Greek, Egyptian, Celtic, and Norse gods and goddesses and invented roles for them on the Internet. They have also invented what they call Web "netiquette," rules for acceptable ritual behavior in cyberspace.

Wiccans are flocking to the Internet in larger numbers all the time, resulting in a large number of Wiccan Web sites. The Witches' Voice Web site features a bulletin board for each state on which neo-Pagan covens and teen, college, and adult groups post their meetings in all fifty states, the United Kingdom, Canada, and in more than forty countries worldwide. There are links to thousands of neo-Pagan Web sites and pages of text. The Witches' Voice also has one of the most extensive lists of occult and metaphysical shops as well as thousands of e-mail addresses for those who hope to network with others who share their beliefs. They sponsor neo-Pagan essay contests and keep abreast of the latest neo-Pagan literature and influences on pop culture. Many Wiccans find much of the information they need about the movement from The Witches' Voice.

Online shopping has also become popular in Wiccan circles. Books, candles, ritual tools, ritual capes, jewelry, and supplies can be bought from many neo-Pagan sites. Other sites sell books only. And one site sells everything from cauldrons to Wiccan greeting cards to books.

If Wicca generates Web traffic, it is only logical that it will generate sales. Penguin Putnam promoted their Sweep series (referred to in the previous section) this way. In their promotional material, they cite a poll from a teen Web site where Wicca ranked as "the second most popular religion after Christianity."

As the Internet fostered the growth of neo-Paganism and book sales grew, it was only a matter of time before Hollywood would want to cash in on these trends.

WITCHCRAFT IN POPULAR ENTERTAINMENT

Witches have long been a part of Western literature and entertainment, including Shakespeare's portrayal of witches in his play *Macbeth*. In recent decades the sitcom *Bewitched*, starring Elizabeth Montgomery as Samantha Stephens, the housewife with magical powers, was popular, and in 2005 Sony Pictures released a remake starring Nicole Kidman as Samantha. *I Dream of Jeannie* was about a genie who used her magical powers to disrupt her master's normal routine. Neither of these sitcoms had anything to do with neo-Paganism, but they did both feature strong women with power, which is, of course, what draws some women to neo-Paganism.

The National Film Board of Canada (NFB), a public agency that produces and distributes films, produced a series of three videos in the early 1990s called the Women and Spirituality series: *Goddess Remembered, The Burning Times,* and *Full Circle.* Respectively, they are about the myth of matriarchal prehistory, the European witch persecutions, and the viability of Goddess spirituality. NFB's New York representative told me, "That trilogy has been our biggest seller in the last ten to fifteen years and continues to be a big seller."

Then, in 1996, Columbia Pictures produced *The Craft.* Starring Neve Campbell and Fairuza Balk, the movie prominently features Wiccan themes. It depicts four lonely teenage girls at a private Los Angeles school who are banished from the popular crowd. The girls form a secret coven, thus representing the four elements, according to the film, that are necessary for magic in witchcraft: north (earth), south (fire), east (air), and west (water). At first their spells have no effect, but soon the girls tap into a powerful way to get what they had long been denied: attention, praise, and love. When their spells begin to work, the coven of girls begins to exact revenge on friends and family, ultimately with disastrous consequences.

A member of Covenant of the Goddess was a consultant on the film, and she tried to educate the producers about Wicca and make the film as authentic as possible. Although some neo-Pagans thought the film was terrible, it was very successful at the box office with one million people see-ing the film on its opening weekend[6]—meaning that many American teenagers were exposed to Wicca in a way they had not been previously.

After *The Craft* came a series of films and TV programs that featured women using magical powers. In *Practical Magic,* Nicole Kidman and Sandra Bullock play sister witches who have to cast some spells to save lives and find true love. The sister theme continued in *Charmed* in which three sisters with magical powers live together in an inherited mansion in San Francisco. *Sabrina the Teenage Witch* features a young girl who has inher-ited magical powers she must keep secret. In neo-Pagan chat rooms, these programs got poor reviews; one reviewer at The Witches' Voice disliked *Charmed* because of its promotion of some biblical themes!

Buffy the Vampire Slayer always seemed to rate more highly than other programs among the Wiccans I interviewed. Buffy is a sixteen-year-old with powers over demons, darkness, and vampires. While the story line is not based on Paganism, the series is not hostile to Wicca, and it portrays a Wiccan friend of Buffy's named Willow in a favorable light.

While none of these films or TV programs are explicitly neo-Pagan, I met many teenagers who were prompted to investigate further after watch-ing them. Most went right to the Internet.

SELLING WICCA

Ironically, neo-Paganism appeals to people because it doesn't seem to be very commercialized. One Pagan woman told me, "People are turning to Paganism for many reasons. The main ones are they are tired of the judg-mental hypocrisy of commercialized religions and want the freedom Pagan-ism gives." But as we can see at the local bookstore, on the Internet, or on our TV sets, Wicca is far from uncommercialized. For example, Wiccans today often charge a fee for passing their knowledge on to younger generations. On the northern coast of California, children ages eight to fourteen can attend Granny Z's Witches and Wizards Camp, run by feminist witch and Goddess worshiper Zsuzsanna Budapest. For $325, parents can drop their children off for four days of horseback riding, archery, swimming, and canoeing, as well as lessons in alchemy, the creation of their own magic tools, and identification of magic rocks and crystals.

There are adult versions of these camps as well. Starhawk's Reclaiming Movement, which links feminist spirituality with a commitment to political and social change, runs witch camps both in the United States and abroad.[7] Interested travelers can also join an international Goddess tour—to Greece or Malta, for example—where neo-Pagan tour guides lead spiritual retreats.

And if an aspiring Wiccan cannot find what she needs to know about Wicca at the bookstore, on the Internet, at witch camps, or on an international Goddess tour, there is an alternative: Wiccan high priestesses and priests offer courses in Wicca. These classes are hosted in people's homes, at community centers, in shops, or at retreat centers. For example, The Craft—Ongoing Wicca 101 course is offered to interested parties in Richmond, Virginia. For $150, participants learn the basics of Wicca, and they receive a meditation kit, a beginner's packet of information, and refreshments. The class is designed especially for the newcomer to Wicca. Their advertisement reads, "Topics covered will include: What is Wicca? how to meditate and achieve ritual consciousness, the Sabbats, Esbats, and spell craft."[8]

Much like Christian preachers, neo-Pagans have also joined the speaker's circuit. M. Macha Nightmare offers two lectures, based on her book *The Pagan Book of Living and Dying*, titled "Meeting Death and

Grieving Loss" and "Healing Ourselves and Healing Our Community." The cost for both talks is $75 to $125 per person. Starhawk holds workshops and speaks all over the world. She also leads tours of the British Isles and offers witchcamps abroad.

Zsuzsanna Budapest also travels and speaks about Goddess spirituality. Her personal Web site provides contact information for those interested in booking her for speaking engagements. She oversees a Biannual Goddess Festival that costs participants between $175 and $350.

The commercialization of neo-Pagan witchcraft has resulted in its entrance into the popular culture, and Christians cannot ignore it because it will inevitably cross their path or the path of family members.

SERIOUS BUSINESS

The consistent message I got from the publishers and marketers of neo-Pagan items, such as books and spell kits, was that they didn't think that what they were promoting was real or could have any effect on impressionable young people.

But that is not what I heard from older neo-Pagans. One woman in Northern Virginia told me, "What those teenagers are doing with Wicca and those books and spell kits really frightens me. They do not know what they are playing with, and it's serious."

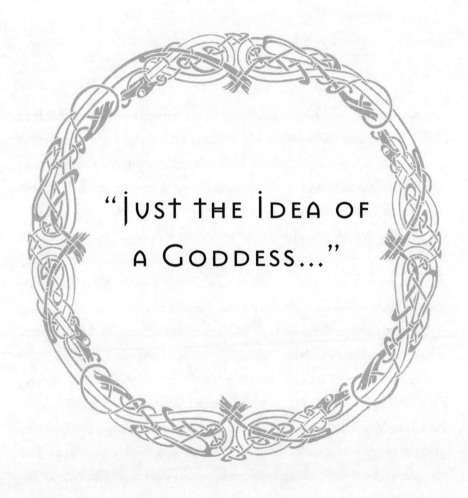

"Just the Idea of a Goddess..."

Women and Wicca

A s I mentioned earlier, according to the best estimates, two-thirds of neo-Pagans are women. Many practice Goddess worship, which is a form of neo-Pagan spirituality with historical roots in feminism. Practitioners worship the Mother Goddess, and, like Wiccans, they believe that the Mother Goddess is a metaphor for the earth. They believe she was present at the dawn of time. Individual goddesses worshiped by Wiccans are believed to be manifestations of the Mother Goddess. Goddess worshipers encourage every woman to view herself as divine—the Goddess incarnate—which is also consistent with neo-Paganism.

What motivates these women? What tugs at their hearts and makes them embrace Goddess worship and Wicca? To find out I attended a women's spirituality conference at a Unity church in Seattle. Those gathered were among a growing segment of women in the Pacific Northwest interested in neo-Paganism. When I entered I noticed large tables outside the meeting sanctuary displaying art, crafts, books on Wicca and Goddess worship, and brochures advertising conference workshops and local neo-Pagan rituals.

When all were seated for the opening keynote address, a hush fell over the sanctuary and the lights were dimmed. Then, at the back of the church, drumming and stomping began, and a group of brightly clothed dancers meandered down the aisle, yelping as they came. Pulsing to the music, they thrust their bodies forward and backward to the beat. Two women leaped out front as if they were dancing on coals of fire. And then the chant began: "We all come from the Goddess, and to her we shall return." These lyrics were penned by Goddess worshiper Zsuzsanna Budapest. The song refers to the Mother Goddess who, according to myth, was worshiped by the ancients.

As the group neared the front, they continued their whooping and hollering, then the drums were struck a final time, and everything stopped. Silence was followed by vigorous applause as women rose to their feet.

The keynote speaker for the evening was prominent witch and author Margot Adler. In 1979 she wrote what many consider to be a defining work on neo-Paganism: *Drawing Down the Moon: Witches, Druids, Goddess-Worshippers, and Other Pagans in America Today.* Adler is also a correspondent on National Public Radio in New York and the granddaughter of one of the twentieth century's important intellectuals, psychologist Alfred Adler. In her remarks Adler clarified what motivated so many of the women to be there as she recalled an interview she'd had with a woman while doing research for her book.

"Just the idea of a Goddess," the woman told her, "[and] I felt this great weight drop from me—I felt the last prejudices against my female body falling away."[1]

For me, that statement put the whole Goddess movement—and much of the interest in Wicca—in a very clear light.

CAROL'S STORY

Carol Christ is a devoted follower of the Goddess and a scholar of the Goddess movement. Her religious experiences provide an example of what Adler was talking about. I heard her speak at a conference called "Religion and the Feminist Movement"at Harvard Divinity School.

Carol's story, as she told it at Harvard, is that after graduation from

Stanford University, she was admitted to Yale Divinity School as the second female PhD candidate in the school's history. She spent countless hours among the library stacks where the only restrooms were for men, and she soon began to feel very isolated as a woman. She was tall and blond, and as she would enter the dining hall, the men in training for the ministry would whistle and make comments about her long legs. She spent a lot of her time crying, she said, feeling that she was appreciated only for her looks rather than her intellect.

Carol's faith in God did not deepen at divinity school. In fact, while there she saw very little of God or his grace in the people around her. Despite attending church on a regular basis, she began to associate the church with discrimination against women as a result of her experience at Yale. Female friends introduced her to feminist consciousness-raising groups, and she began to learn that many feminists had jettisoned God altogether and had instead embraced a goddess.[2]

Carol has since become a prolific author. In one of her books, she writes,

For me and for many others, finding the Goddess has felt like coming home to a vision of life that we had always known deeply within ourselves: that we are part of nature and that our destiny is to participate fully in the cycles of birth, death, and renewal that characterize life on this earth. We find in the Goddess a compelling image of female power, a vision of the deep connection of all beings in the web of life, and a call to create peace on earth.[3]

Inspired by the quote, "I found God within myself, and I loved her fiercely," Carol left the church and ran headlong into the embrace of neo-Pagan Goddess spirituality. She taught at various American universities before she became frustrated with academia and decided to move to Greece. Today she gives academic lectures worldwide and leads women pilgrims on Goddess spirituality tours to ancient pagan sites in Greece and Turkey.

Roots of Wicca and Goddess Worship

As Carol's story illustrates, as feminism grew, so did Goddess worship and Wicca. But what is the history of Goddess worship, and how is it intertwined with Wicca? As I learned in Salem, Wiccans and Goddess worshipers feel solidarity with those who were accused of witchcraft and were executed hundreds of years ago. Wicca's emphasis on self-empowerment, often through supernatural means, and matriarchal deism (which I'll discuss in more detail later) was appealing to feminists. They began to call their spiritual movement "women's spirituality." It was a spontaneous, grassroots movement with no overarching organization, system of leadership, or membership. Its primary characteristic was and still is variety.

The most important area of agreement among participants is that their spirituality is uniquely empowering for women. Whatever works to make a woman stronger is the goal.[4] In keeping with neo-Pagan philosophy, there is a deep interest in ritual as a tool of empowerment and in some form of magic, divination, or cultivation of psychic skills. Nature is revered and often worshiped and personified as the Mother Goddess—or Mother Earth. Women, too, are revered for their female biological functions, such as childbirth and menstruation. The goal is personal empowerment, regardless of what it takes.

Much of the women's spirituality movement got its start with consciousness-raising groups, active in the 1960s and 1970s, in which women were encouraged to discuss what being a woman in American culture entailed. The typical gathering consisted of a group of women who would sit in a circle and select a topic for discussion. Because many women in attendance felt they had no voice in society, each was permitted to speak on the topic without interruption, criticism, or praise.

Political feminism sought to provide women an outlet for their frustration with equality under the law, but this did not satisfy the spiritual hunger many felt. In the minds of some feminists, the one area that appeared to be dominated by men was established religion—usually Christianity and the institution of the church. In talking with many of these women, I found that the majority who embraced Goddess spirituality had grown up attending church. Some theologians and many ordinary congregants had developed an unhealthy skepticism toward the supernatural. So, many who were looking for a supernatural experience at that time moved toward the occult.[5] Christians who believed in the supernatural and might have had some interesting things to share with these women about grace and the power of God's love largely steered clear of such feminist gatherings. By the 1970s the first covens had been established in the United States. Gardnerian witchcraft's focus on the Goddess and on the matriarchal myth (which we'll examine in detail next) appealed to feminists, and they were hooked.*

THE MATRIARCHAL MYTH

For many years proponents of modern witchcraft have promoted a view of history that claims a lineage stretching back to European witches, and even

---

* There were indications of neo-Paganism among the early feminists, the suffragettes. See the appendix for more information about neo-Paganism's influence on L. Frank Baum's *The Wizard of Oz*.

further back to prehistoric times. There has always been some division within neo-Pagan circles about the authenticity of this theory, and although not all Pagans believe it, many do.

In her 1979 book *The Spiral Dance: The Rebirth of the Ancient Religion of the Great Goddess,* Starhawk was among several authors at the time who wrote about this myth and catalyzed a generation into the practice of neo-Pagan witchcraft. You read variations of it in many books about Wicca, but this is basically how it goes:

Witchcraft began in Paleolithic times when people worshiped the goddess of the earth and the god of the hunt, the Horned God. The Mother Goddess was the great life-giver. The first covens were formed. These Goddess-worshiping cultures were peaceful matriarchal societies and existed for thousands of years. Then Indo-European warrior tribes, who worshiped male warrior gods and were dominated by men, invaded and conquered these Goddess worshipers.

After these tribes invaded, the marriage of the warrior gods to the goddesses took place, and the great temple of the gods at Olympus was created. It was the same among other peoples, such as the ancient Egyptians and the Celts and Nordic peoples, all of whom worshiped gods and goddesses. After this invasion, life for the peace-loving goddess communities was never quite the same. They were persecuted by the stronger patriarchal communities.

The arrival of Christianity brought about little change in the lives of these communities. Leaders and kings were converted, but the people continued to worship their pagan gods and goddesses. Some began to worship both pagan gods and the Christian God. But soon, much of Europe began to convert to Christianity. Pagan temples were demolished, and Christian churches were built on top of these sites.[6]

Soon the Goddess worshipers were driven underground, forced to practice their religion in secret. They were called witches, benders, and shapers of Nature, who was the Mother Goddess they worshiped and asked to do things for them. They resurfaced occasionally throughout history, such as during the witch trials of medieval Europe.

The witches continued to be outcasts from society, but faithful practitioners kept this "old religion" alive, and in the mid-1950s, when the witchcraft laws were repealed in England, they became more public.[7]

Today Goddess worshipers claim to be making a comeback. Since women dominate the practice, they say that they are reclaiming their heritage, hoping to return our world to the peaceful, Goddess-worshiping, female-dominated matriarchal community it once was.

This myth can be heard at feminist gatherings, in Women's Studies programs, at neo-Pagan festivals, and from Wiccans themselves. The myth has been circulated widely and reverently.

In his book *Earth in the Balance,* even former vice president Al Gore pondered the validity of the matriarchal myth and mentions the notion of a "single earth goddess" worshiped throughout "prehistoric Europe and much of the world" replaced by later religions with their "distinctly masculine orientation." Gore does acknowledge, however, that the evidence and "elaborate and imaginative analysis used to interpret the artifacts leave much room for skepticism about our ability to know exactly what this belief system...taught."[8]

Recently every part of this matriarchal myth has been challenged by historians. Adler herself told the women in Seattle that there was no way the matriarchal myth could be proven. In an essay on Beliefnet.com titled "A Time for Truth," Adler goes even further:

During the past 10 years, there has been what Ronald Hutton, in his recent book *The Triumph of the Moon,* calls a "tidal wave of accumulating research" that has essentially swept away many of the assumptions upon which the "Old Religion," Wicca, was based. Two of the most basic that have been revised are the notion of an unbroken tradition and the belief that our religion had a history of persecution that rivaled or even exceeded the Jewish Holocaust....

If scholarship is redrawing the picture of the Burning Times, it is also reconfiguring the origins of Wicca. Scholars have never accepted the myth of an unbroken Wiccan tradition, and now most Wiccans are being asked to look honestly at their history....

This new breeze that is blowing through Wicca is not being celebrated by the more literal among us. In some groups, there is open hostility to this revisionist history.[9]

The matriarchal myth has attracted thousands of women to the practice of witchcraft and Goddess spirituality over the past three decades. It gave credence and historical context to Wicca for many adherents, and it should come as no surprise that many are hostile to the new scholarship. Adler also writes in her essay that it is not surprising that feminists promoted this myth as it became a "way to express rage at the misogyny of contemporary culture."[10]

Other Pagans echo Adler. Medieval historian and Wiccan Jenny Gibbons wrote an excellent article in 1998 for the neo-Pagan publication *The Pomegranate,* in which she notes the influence of feminist writings on the Wiccan myth and how many of them have long distorted reality. She writes,

In 1973, Barbara Ehrenreich and Deirdre English suggested that most witches were mid-wives and female healers. Their book *Witches, Midwives, and Nurses* convinced many feminists and Pagans that the Great Hunt was a pogrom aimed at traditional women healers. The Church and State sought to break the power of these women by accusing them of witchcraft, driving a wedge of fear between the wise-woman and her clients. The evidence for this theory was—and is—completely anecdotal. Authors cited a number of cases involving healers, then simply assumed that this was what the "average" trial was like. However a mere decade after *Witches, Midwives, and Nurses* was published, we knew that this was not true. Healers made up a small percentage of the accused, usually between 2% and 20%, depending on the country. There was never a time or a place where the majority of accused witches were healers.[11]

In actual fact, if a woman was a licensed midwife, this actually decreased her chance of being charged.[12]

Oxford University historian Robin Briggs wrote a thorough study of historical witchcraft in 1996 titled *Witches and Neighbors*. After extensive primary-source research, Briggs concluded that most of the European witch trials took place from 1450 to 1750, during the time of the harshest capital punishments in Europe, and mostly in modern-day France, Switzerland, and Germany—areas already embroiled in religious turmoil because of the Protestant Reformation. Many of the witch trials, which Briggs estimates numbered one hundred thousand, occurred among the poor and unpopular of the local population—quite different from the independent-minded women they have been portrayed to be by neo-Pagans. One-quarter of the forty to fifty thousand executed were actually men. Briggs also found no record that any of the accused were executed because they practiced an ancient pagan religion.[13]

Since these recent historical developments have discredited common thinking about the history of modern witchcraft, I was surprised to learn that, for many Wiccans, Wiccan history does not matter. After an article on Goddess worship appeared in the *Atlantic Monthly*, Starhawk wrote in a letter to the editor,

> Goddess religion is not based on history, archaeology, or belief
> in any Great Goddess past or present. Our spirituality is based
> on experience, on a direct relationship with the cycles of birth,
> growth, death, and regeneration in nature and in human lives.
> We see the complex, interwoven web of life as sacred, which
> is to say real and important, worth protecting, worth taking a
> stand for.[14]

While truth about men's mistreatment of women or the discriminatory history of Christianity seems to matter greatly to neo-Pagans, the truth about their own history does not. What matters more to them is experience and how their spirituality makes them feel.

ORIGINS OF THE MATRIARCHAL MYTH

So Wicca and its spiritual cousin, Goddess worship, were thrust into the American mainstream largely because of feminism. What many female seekers might not realize is that many of the ideas of matriarchal Goddess culture and the roots of Wicca, surprisingly, were pioneered by Victorian men.

57

Karl Ernst Jarcke and Franz Josef Mone

The early nineteenth century provided fertile ground for ideas about neo-Paganism to be born and flourish. This was the era of the Romantic poets, of revering nature in art and literature. After all, neo-Paganism greatly romanticizes nature. During this period, two German-Catholic scholars, Karl Ernst Jarcke and Franz Josef Mone, first identified witches as Pagans. Jarcke first theorized that the witchcraft of European history was a form of ancient paganism. Jarcke believed that an ancient pagan religion had lingered among the people, and the practitioners had been condemned as Satanists and witches and were forced to the periphery of society. Both scholars proposed that these "witches" were a throwback to a matriarchal golden age and were merely following the ancient pagan religions of their foremothers. This interpretation was entirely new, and Jarcke did not support this theory with any evidence.[15]

Jules Michelet and J. J. Bachofen

Victorian French historian Jules Michelet nonetheless took up this theme. He believed that Christianity had to give way to a new faith better suited to the new age, a faith built around the notion of motherhood. Michelet wrote several books, including three volumes on the history of France and one, *La Sorcière,* in which he promoted Jarcke's theory that witchcraft was a surviving pagan fertility cult. Michelet was an early adopter of the theory of a universal, ancient Mother Goddess.[16]

Soon another book appeared, this time by a Swiss-German historian named Johann Jakob Bachofen titled *Myth, Religion, and Mother Right.* The "Mother Right" would also have a profound influence on the creation of modern Wicca, Goddess worship, and women's spirituality. Bachofen asserted that the first societies of history were matriarchal and that ancients worshiped the Mother Goddess. In Bachofen's view, this golden matriarchal age came to an end when male invaders, bearing a solar religion, defeated the matriarchy with its lunar orientation. Sound familiar?

Most of Bachofen's theories have been discredited in his field of ancient history, but they gained currency in radical politics, literature, and psychology. He himself acknowledged that he did not adhere to the traditional rules of archaeology when proposing the theory of matriarchy. It is worth noting that Bachofen, in fact, adored his own mother. Her death no doubt prompted his vision of a golden time—the Mother Right or matriarchy— where mothers would rule.[17]

Margaret Murray's Speculation

This theme was again appropriated in the early twentieth century by Margaret Murray, a well-known archaeologist and specialist in Egyptian hieroglyphics at University College, London. In 1921 Murray wrote a book titled *Witch Cult in Western Europe* in which she claimed that the persecution of witches in Europe was an attack of the patriarchal establishment on ancient, woman-centered religions. A second book, *God of the Witches,* was published in 1933.

In *Witch Cult* Murray examined the European witch trials to understand the characteristics of the accused. Her explanation was that there was an ancient underground nature religion that originated in pre-Christian Europe.[18] These witches worshiped the "horned male god," and their leader dressed up in an animal costume, often with antlers on his head, and was treated as an incarnation of the male counterpart to the Mother Goddess. Murray believed that Christians had labeled this leader "the devil" because of his horned appearance, so when witches confessed to meeting the devil, they were in reality referring to their leader.[19] This theory was understandably controversial at the time, but even more so was Murray's hypothesis that the witch cult performed human and animal sacrifice, something that modern witches vehemently deny.[20]

In another part of *Witch Cult,* Murray asserted that witches were highly placed in the court of King James VI and used magic in an attempt to poison him so they could install their own leader, the Earl of Bothwell, on the throne.[21] At the conference in Seattle, Adler referred to this theory as "harebrained."

Murray popularized the terminology that is familiar to most modern covens—*sabbats* and *esbats,* the days when the witch cult performs their seasonal and lunar rituals. In her book *Drawing Down the Moon,* Adler writes that most scholars find Murray's work filled with errors. Despite the questionable reliability of her research, however, it is clear that Murray's books have become the basis for modern neo-Pagan witchcraft and deserve serious scrutiny by modern Wiccans.

Gerald Gardner

No discussion about Wicca would be complete without explaining the influence of Gerald Gardner. It was Gardner who, in the middle of the twentieth century, gathered together all of these themes and created what we know today as Wicca.

While living in South Asia, he became very interested in folklore and magical traditions, so he acquainted himself with local tribes and published a study on a Malayan ceremonial knife called the *kris.* Gardner was a Freemason, interested in Asian philosophy, sunbathing, magic, and nudism.

After retiring to England in the mid-1930s, Gardner kept up his Masonic connections and indulged his love for the human body by becoming involved in a nudist club in the New Forest in the south of England.

According to one of his biographers, while walking in the New Forest one day, Gardner stumbled across a group who called themselves an authentic coven of witches. Gardner was fascinated with them and claimed to have been initiated into their coven in 1939.[22] Gardner soon became a practicing witch.

In England in 1951 the repeal of the Witchcraft and Vagrancy Acts enabled witches to practice publicly, which Gardner did, and he also granted frequent press interviews.[23]

Gardner wrote *High Magic's Aid* in 1949 from information that, according to Adler, he learned in a novel,[24] and in 1951 he wrote two books, *Witchcraft Today* and *The Meaning of Witchcraft*. Gardner began to lead many covens himself, retreated to the Isle of Man, and even opened a Museum of Witchcraft there. Today, Gardnerian witchcraft is practiced widely in the West. Aidan Kelly argues that all organized witchcraft in the West merits the title "Gardnerian." Some witches operate in a direct line of Gardnerian imitation, while others define themselves in opposition to it. But almost all types of witchcraft use elements found in Gardner's work. The word *Wicca* itself became popular when Gardner began using it instead of *witchcraft*. Linguists quarrel over its meaning. Some say it means "to bend or shape." Gardner defined the word as "wise one." Strict Gardnerians worship nude and practice ritual scourging to raise magical power. These actions clearly reflect Gardner's own personal proclivities.

Gardner was heavily influenced by Margaret Murray's theories in *Witch Cult in Western Europe* and borrowed her terminology of esbats and sabbats. He also adopted her belief that witches throughout history were members of a pagan sect that worshiped the Horned God.

Other parts of Gardner's rituals were adopted from the Masons. He created what Wiccans call their *Book of Shadows*—their magical diary.

Doreen Valiente, an initiate into Gardner's coven, noted that an article about shadow divination in India appeared in England in 1949. Gardner likely borrowed the phrase from there.[25]

Gardner added his own preference for nudity into some of the rites. Today, Wiccans use a ceremonial knife called an *athame,* which could have been appropriated from the Malayan knives Gardner studied at great length.

So how did Wicca, an obscure spirituality practiced by a flamboyant man on England's remote Isle of Man, make its way to the United States? An English initiate of a Gardner coven, Raymond Buckland, was born in England but settled on Long Island and established the first coven in the United States in the 1960s. Buckland, who is still active, has written thirty books since then and considers himself an expert on witchcraft and the occult. He was responsible for initiating Margot Adler into the Gardnerian tradition, and shortly thereafter she completed *Drawing Down the Moon.*

Aleister Crowley

Called the "enfant terrible of early twentieth-century magic" by Wiccan high priestess Phyllis Curott, Aleister Crowley lived during the first half of the twentieth century.[26] His behavior was always colorful, flamboyant, and often shocking. He is commonly associated with modern sex magic in which intercourse is seen as a way to tap into the creative energy of all couples.

Crowley and Gardner met in the late 1940s, shortly before Crowley's death. Gardner appropriated some of Crowley's rituals for his own witchcraft, and extensive verbatim passages from Crowley's works appear in Gardner's early witchcraft rituals. According to a biography of Gardner, Crowley himself, however, declined to enter the witch religion because he didn't want to be "bossed around" by women.[27]

While Crowley may not have had much respect for women, he certainly enjoyed them sexually. As an undergraduate at Cambridge University, he displayed a voracious sexual appetite and later wrote in his diary about how, even in his sixties, he would prowl the streets of London looking for sex.

In his book *Magick in Theory and Practice,* Crowley cites one of his favorite sayings from French writer Rabelais: "Do what thou wilt shall be the whole of the law," which Wiccans have adapted and called the Wiccan Rede, "Do what you will and [you] harm none." In his book *The Law Is for All,* Crowley argues that children should be required to observe sexual activity.[28]

Crowley's writings became the basis for much of his ritual magic. He established a magical commune in Sicily, but Mussolini expelled him in 1923 for lurid behavior.

Although Crowley's personal behavior and comments were somewhat demeaning to women, in his writings he did recognize a female deity: the Mother Goddess.[29] Gardner also appropriated many of Crowley's ritual tools, now commonly used in Wicca today: the sword, the dagger, the wand, the censer, the pentacle, and the scourge.[30] According to Aidan Kelly, Doreen Valiente rewrote much of Crowley's ritual for Gardner to make it a bit less sensational.[31]

Whether or not they like what Crowley wrote, Wiccans have to recognize that he influenced their belief system. As the New Age journal *Gnosis* acknowledges, "If you're interested in magic as a spiritual discipline, you must deal with Crowley."[32]

Wicca Is Recent History

Since the birth of the modern feminist movement, the matriarchal-myth theory has developed and gained ground among Wiccans and feminists, forming an elaborate spirituality. While Wicca originated in England, Goddess spirituality was adopted and promoted as a by-product of the feminist movement in the United States.

Historian Ronald Hutton notes that compared to ancient European religions and archaeological evidence, contemporary Wiccan rituals and the language of modern magic spells have no roots prior to 1900. Over time the rituals and practices espoused in Gardner's work have been adopted by Wiccans even though his witchcraft texts were his personal creation and not something handed to him from an ancient tradition. Wicca is not a revival of an ancient pagan religion, but a modern invention. This is in stark contrast to Christianity, which has its roots in the ancient world and draws on more than six thousand years of Hebrew Scriptures.

A MYTH DOES NOT HAVE TO BE TRUE TO BE MEANINGFUL

Despite Adler's and other neo-Pagans' claims that the myth of matriarchal prehistory has no basis in fact, the reality that it is still embraced shows how much some women are longing for something more than what many have received at church and perceive to be Christianity. A myth does not have to be true to be meaningful. People are also looking for a deity they can control—a god who suits their valid, real needs when they feel that Christianity cannot.

The Need for Dignity

I met a woman named Amber at the Beltane festival who called herself a lapsed Methodist and a Dianic witch, which means that she identifies with Diana, the Roman goddess of the hunt. As Ginny in Asheville had told me, many, but not all, Dianic witches are lesbians and "left-wing ladies." After twenty-five years of marriage, Amber divorced her husband and turned to witchcraft.

Soon after we met, her anger toward men was apparent as she denounced them all as wanting their wives to be barefoot and pregnant.

"We only need three men on the earth! As women we can take care of everything else," she laughed. "Witchcraft has always been a woman's thing. Women knew how to heal the community…until the patriarchy took away our powers," she continued, her eyes flashing.

Amber did not know if Diana was a Roman or a Greek goddess. She only knew that those who worshiped her were against men, the "patriarchy" she sees as dominating society.

"Some Dianics want a totally matriarchal society and want to bring the 'patriarchy' down—I mean all the way to the ground," she told me. "I don't go quite that far, but I am against the patriarchy."

In Virginia, Amber gathers with other Dianics at a place in the Tidewater region known as the House of the Goddess or, by its longer name, Artemis Reborn's House of the Goddess—Center for Pagan Wombyn. Their Web site features a spider crawling across the screen and announcements that they practice "feminist politix" and reestablishment of "matristic societies." They have "Hot Goddess" potluck suppers and give visitors free literature on feminist spirituality.

"The people at the House of the Goddess let no man enter—not even a recorded male voice," Amber told me. "When I was there we played a CD with a man's voice on it, and it was taken out of the house."

While these actions seem somewhat extreme, the anger that many of the women who embrace the Goddess direct toward the patriarchy is not without justification. We have to be honest and acknowledge that men have mistreated women over the centuries, and nothing excuses this behavior. Some women over the years have been taught to take a backseat to the men, to get their self-worth from their husbands alone, to give boys the best of life's opportunities. Women are right to mourn over this mistreatment. This type of patriarchal behavior is sinful. We cannot blame only the men, however, as such behavior has been encouraged by women, too. Both sexes can be blamed for allowing mistreatment inside the church as well.

But as we consider past mistakes, we must be very careful not to equate God with the male rule, the patriarchy that has existed for millennia on earth. Many women embrace the Goddess because they believe that God is male and exactly like the men they know. However, the Hebrew Scriptures have long taught that God transcends gender. Scripture emphasizes that God is not an earthly creature but is wholly "other."[33] Nonetheless, over the centuries, men and women have given creaturely attributes to God and have perceived God as male alone. Because of this, many women have felt frustrated. So it is not difficult to understand why a whole industry of Goddess merchandise has been built up around Goddess spirituality.

A few years ago I even came across a "Go Goddess!" board game that retails for fifty dollars, comes packaged in a colorful hat box, and has decks of cards with thought-provoking questions, a wheel of light, and seven candles. The downstairs at the Women of Wisdom Conference was itself a "Goddess market" where vendors could peddle such wares. Many women at the conference were clutching copies of the newsletter *Goddessing Regenerated,* whose "cauldron of events" on the entire front page listed international Goddess tours going everywhere from Ireland to Peru.

With its lack of doctrinal orthodoxy, Wicca lends itself to perpetual telling of the matriarchal myth. Since one of Wicca's highest values is supernatural experience, a woman may feel she has experienced the Goddess worshiped by the ancients despite all the historical knowledge that one

Goddess did not exist. She simply believes that there is a supernatural force that exists that is not the God of the Bible. Through divination, tarot cards, and various other methods, women are able to tap into this unseen, supernatural spirit world that is all too real for them.

The Need for Ritual

One of the most appealing aspects of neo-Paganism for women is its emphasis on rite and ritual. Adler's love for witchcraft, for example, was a by-product of her longing for some sort of religious ritual in her life.

As a child Adler had been raised in what she called a Jewish-Marxist-atheist home. Because no faith was practiced in her home, she longed for a faith of her own and was jealous of the liturgy and ritual experienced by her Catholic friends during Mass. When she was ten she participated in an Old English May Day ceremony at school, where she and her classmates arose before dawn to pick flowers, returned to school, and strewed them about the classrooms. After this experience, she told the group in Seattle, she became a "ritual junkie for life."[34] In the 1960s, Adler became a witch.

The Seattle audience oohed and aahed when she spoke about her May Day ritual celebrating spring. It is an ancient pagan pre-Christian holiday. After living through a gray English winter, I could understand the need to celebrate. In fact, when Adler spoke, what she said was very familiar to me.

Growing up outside of Oxford, England, my friends and I would get up early on the first of May when it was still dark and join with thousands of Oxford students and townspeople as we welcomed spring with the sunrise. The name of the celebration in Oxford is, in fact, May Morning. The choirboys from Magdalen College would sing hymns of praise, thanking God for the new season in the tradition of the early Christians in England who acknowledged the pagan holiday and love of nature and simply thanked God for it. The tradition continues today. The choirboys weren't the only ones to celebrate, however.

Traditional English Morris dancers performed in the streets, and hundreds of drunken students paraded around town, uncorking champagne bottles and jumping off bridges into the river Thames! As typical fifteen-year-olds, we girls enjoyed the festive atmosphere.

I have very fond memories of those mornings when the sun would rise and all you could hear was the boys choir. Using a change in season to thank God was always a moving, earthy experience for me.

Modern American society isn't old enough to have developed such celebrations. Secular America is so denuded of religion, ritual, and nature that it is not surprising that Adler would find this ritual thirst quenching.

The Need for Rites of Passage

Women throughout history have felt undervalued and overworked in many aspects of their lives—as mothers, wives, friends, in the community, and in their careers. Spiritually adrift, they seek a safe harbor where they feel appreciated and accepted. Many women who feel disenfranchised from the political process and the business world and marginalized at church gravitate toward celebrating their status as women instead.

As women we have always been aware of our bodies' unique functions: menstruation, childbirth, and menopause. But in the West we lack rituals to mark the passage of time in women's lives and changes in their bodies. Our society does not always provide room to laugh and weep over the cycles of life. Wicca offers rituals for the living and dying times of life.

In Wicca the cycles of the moon are seen to represent women's monthly cycles. Central to neo-Paganism is acknowledgment of the connection be-tween our bodies and nature. Laura and Donna, the women I interviewed at the Beltane festival, explained the importance of these Wiccan rites of passage.

"We celebrate three phases of life. For women there are three phases of the Goddess: maiden, mother, and crone," Laura told me. "For men there are three phases of the god: green man, oak king, and holly king."

Like much of neo-Paganism, these life phases correspond to the change in seasons. *Maiden* represents a young woman in the springtime of her life.

"It is the breath of fresh air after winter's rest; it is everything coming back; it is renewal," Laura said, her cheeks flushed with excitement as she spoke. "When young children are nine or ten, they have their maidening ceremony."

Girls may also be maidened when they begin menstruation—what Laura called their "moon cycle." Then, when a child is older, she can choose to become a witch.

I read one account of a maidening ceremony of a seventeen-year-old girl whose parents looked on as she undressed in front of the coven and members anointed her with oil, then whipped and kissed her. The girl said she regretted sunbathing the day before because the whipping hurt her back, which was sunburned.

All maidening ceremonies are different, and not all involve whipping. The ritual account I read is largely based on Gardnerian witchcraft. Laura and Donna told me that they follow different paths and do not whip any-one in their covens.

Mother, the second phase of life, represents summertime, according to Laura. "The woman is in full bloom—is fertile and perhaps with child.

Croning occurs when a woman reaches maturity, has stopped her bleeding, and is full of wisdom."

Boys experience the same phases of life. The *green man* is a young boy, the *oak king* is more mature, and the *holly king*—often portrayed by a Santa Claus–type figure—represents a man in the winter of his life, someone who has accomplished much, has great knowledge of witchcraft, and is respected within the community for his wisdom.

Laura and Donna told me they felt it was very important that Wiccans be shepherded through these phases by a group or coven that is committed to supervising them.

"Teenage girls and their spell kits are very scary to me," Laura said. "They have absolutely no idea what they are playing with. Magic is very real and can come back to harm them."

Donna agreed. "When teens do their love spells, they focus their minds on intent. They are changing energy patterns and can affect things; they can indeed change things," she warned.

Wiccans are tapping into the importance of cultural rites of passage, something that has been lost on much of secular Western culture. Throughout history, men and women have been honored at various stages of life. Many cultures honor the elderly for their wisdom. But Americans live in a society that values youth and life and distances itself from the cycles of life and death. The fact that some covens would go so far as to whip participants to mark life's passage shows how desperate many women are to be noticed.

While on assignment in Japan, Peggy Orenstein, a contributing writer to the *New York Times Magazine* and author of *Flux: Women on Sex, Work, Love, Kids, and Life in a Half-Changed World,* wrote a poignant essay about a miscarriage she suffered while covering the new childlessness in the Asian country. Orenstein is Jewish, and she describes very vividly her pain at the loss of this much-wanted child and her desire to use ritual to mark the baby's passing. She looked to ancient Japanese practices and found a ritual for the aborted or miscarried child. She writes,

> There's little acknowledgment in Western culture of miscarriage, no ritual to cleanse the grief. My own religion, Judaism, despite its meticulous attention to the details of daily life, has traditionally been silent on pregnancy loss—on most matters of pregnancy and childbirth, in fact.... Christianity, too, has largely overlooked miscarriage....
>
> It is only if your pregnancy is among the unlucky ones that fail that you begin to hear the stories, spoken in confidence, almost whispered. Your aunt. Your grandmother. Your friends. Your colleagues. Women you have known for years—sometimes your whole life—who have had this happen, sometimes over and over and over again. They tell only if you become one of them....
>
> Americans don't like unhappy endings. We recoil from death....
>
> For days after the miscarriage, I walked around in a gray haze, not knowing what to do with my sadness.[35]

She soon discovered a fourteenth-century temple called Zozo-ji, where it was common to make offerings to Jizo, the "enlightened being" who watches over miscarried fetuses. She bought an armful of toys and arranged them at the feet of the Jizo statue that was adorned with a little knitted red baby bonnet. She said a prayer and asked the monk to chant a lotus sutra for her and the fetus. As she left the temple, she wrote that she was glad she had gone there: "I had done something to commemorate this event; I'd said goodbye. I'm grateful to have had that opportunity."[36]

Orenstein's story tells us that faith as it is often practiced in the West seems to lack the ritual and earthy reality of the Jizo ceremony or other pagan rituals. But I suspect there is more behind a desire for such rites of passage than the act of assuaging a deity. Ritual feeds the human need to do something for ourselves. Ritual allows us to feel that we are doing something. It helps us grieve and is a way God provides healing for our brokenness.

Longing for Eden on Earth

Margot Adler echoed Peggy Orenstein's critique as she spoke in Seattle. She, too, was angry about organized religion.

"Since September 11, I have been in a religious rage," she said. "I think that we are [now] confronted with some very uncomfortable truths about the great religions."

But, as Adler admitted, her own neo-Pagan tradition is fraught with trouble. She settled on experience as the ultimate spiritual guidepost but contradicted herself when she chided women for relying too much on their own experience: "Trusting in one's feelings can sometimes lead one down the road to self-delusion," she told the audience gathered in Seattle. But within neo-Paganism, dissension is clearly tolerated and contradictions are allowed. Adler was typical of other neo-Pagans I met who could hold monotheistic religions to a standard of truth when they displayed no concern for truth in their own spirituality.

She continued: "All three religions—Judaism, Islam, and Christianity—have brought us history fraught with wars, crusades, jihads, rape, and slavery." Saddened by this fact, she had hoped that as modern people we had progressed past such actions.

"But the thing that has put me into the deepest rage and sadness is that I have realized that we are not through that. This has created fear and rage!"

She was almost shaking as she spoke, clutching the microphone. She told us that she wished to create a future society—something that would incorporate ecology, feminism, and science fiction, all things she loved. I understood her desire for a society free of pain—an Eden. Many have tried to create such a place on earth but have failed, and the world continues to be a dire and dirty place, tinged with beauty. This reality made Adler very upset.[37]

What is the answer? Can human striving and ritual change the world and people's hearts? Inscribed on existentialist philosopher Albert Camus's tombstone is a quote from his play *The Myth of Sisyphus:* "The struggle toward the summit itself suffices to fill the heart." Is it really rewarding to push the boulder continually up the hill when we know that the boulder will always roll back down and, despite our striving, will never reach the summit? Is this the best we can hope for—continual striving in the midst of wars and pain?

I don't think that Paganism is going to make all things right. The pagan Greeks and Romans certainly fought their share of wars and treated women and slaves terribly. So for neo-Pagans, the question is whether there is a religion that can overcome our troubled world. Many of the Pagans I met are deeply disillusioned with the reality of living in a sinful world and hope to make it a better place, which is ironically why Christians believe that Christ came to earth, died, and was resurrected. Can Wicca and Goddess worship save us from ourselves? Gently asking this question to a neo-Pagan friend or neighbor or a Wiccan relative could start a fruitful dialogue for both sides. So often it is the people who take time to understand the other side who have a lasting impact.

MAKING A DIFFERENCE

Another woman at the Harvard conference, Roberta Hestenes, had experiences like Carol Christ's. Her story turned out a little differently, however, and it was because Christians took time to be with her.

Roberta became a Christian in her youth. After her conversion she attended a Christian camp one summer on Catalina Island in California and began to lead a Bible study in the local coffee shop in town. Throughout the course of the summer, people in the coffee shop came to know Christ. She was very excited, but soon word of this coffee-shop Bible study filtered to camp leadership, and the men in charge told her that she would no longer be able to lead such a study because she was a woman. A man had to take over. So a man did, and the Bible study soon fizzled. Roberta had several other experiences like this within evangelical circles. She was discouraged, but on more than one occasion, other Christian men and women encouraged her to stick with it. She knew that in the Bible, Jesus had elevated and welcomed women beyond the normal custom of the time. So Roberta persevered and is a faithful Christian today. She was affiliated with World Vision, a Christian relief organization, and in 1987 became the president of a Christian college. Roberta is an example of someone who became a Christian as feminism was on the rise. She and Carol both encountered some hostility because they were women. Carol chose to abandon Christianity, whereas Roberta embraced it. Goddess worship could have appealed to both women. But it was the people who crossed their paths at these times in their lives who made the difference in which way each chose to go.[38]

DOES GOD REALLY
LOVE WOMEN?

The Search for Dignity

Carol's experience and feelings about God and the church echo what many women today feel. Carol's views are by no means uncommon, and they raise a number of questions. Is there a place in the church for women, or is the gospel message one that portrays women as second-class citizens? Do women need to go outside the church to find a religion, such as neo-Paganism, that celebrates their womanhood? Wiccans always say how empowering Wicca is for women. Can Christianity speak to this? In this chapter we'll explore what I believe to be the reality that, while romantic on some level, Wicca and Goddess spirituality offer no special dignity to women. This background may be of help to you as you look for a way to respond to a Wiccan friend or as you compare Wicca and Christianity for yourself.

MARY DALY'S ANSWER

For radical feminist and neo-Pagan Mary Daly, women are the answer to the world's problems. If only women could run everything, things would be so much better. For years her critique has been that the church has nothing for women and has done a terrible job providing a place for them. Is she right?

In the 1960s Daly wrote a book called *The Church and the Second Sex*.

It declares, among other things, that the church, which has been misogynistic since New Testament times, should discard the "perverted" notion that God is immutable. It should embrace the Goddess. Daly rejected Catholic belief early in her career, saying that she found Paganism more attractive and has recommended the worship of pagan goddesses as more beneficial for women than Christianity. After the appearance of Daly's book, Boston College, a Catholic institution, asked her to step down from her teaching position. Her outrage at this request rallied thousands of students to her cause. During what must have been a colorful seven-hour "teach-in," local self-described witches came and hexed Boston College. The college relented and granted Daly tenure and a promotion. Daly mockingly labeled this move as evidence of patriarchal cowardice.

Daly spoke at a Harvard conference and dedicated her speech to her cats—which she called her "familiars"—to "slobbering husbands," and to the Jesuits at "St. Pedophilia's" church, and she insulted Boston College, "that jock school," where she no longer taught.[1] Daly was known for years as a brilliant Catholic scholar, and I must admit that her speech that night was clever and entertaining, although completely incoherent. At the end of the conference, my friend Lilian Calles Barger, founder of the Damaris Project, an organization in dialogue with feminist spirituality, asked Daly a question. Curious as to how Daly saw her worldview being lived out in daily life, Barger asked Daly how she, for example, would apply what she had just said to her life back home on Monday morning when she returned to her husband and two sons.

Daly told her that her husband and sons were the problem. Daly has also famously said that "if God is male, then male is God." Men are the problem, and the gospel is certainly not the answer as far as she is concerned.

IT'S THE CULTURE, NOT THE GOSPEL

I met with similar responses throughout my travels. But I found that the fallen, sinful human condition, which leads to the cultural objectification of women, seemed to be the real culprit rather than the message of the gospel.

Women as Objects

Thirteen-year-old Sarah embraced Wicca because she shared Mary Daly's frustrations with the state of affairs in this world. She wasn't happy with the status quo and perceived the church as often being a hypocritical accomplice to the world's ills. She told me that most of her school friends were too shallow, airy, and thoughtless. Unconcerned with deeper issues such as religion, they filled their days with talk of boys and school and makeup. Sarah desired something more serious and discovered that those like-minded students in her class happened to be Wiccan. So Sarah began to practice Wicca. Sarah was bright and did well in school, and because of her intellectual curiosity, she began to investigate the origins of Wicca. Unlike many teens, Sarah was dismayed when she realized that Wicca was not an ancient religion, but that it had all come about rather recently as the creation of a group of English men and women.

"Then I saw *The Craft*," she told me. "What a ridiculous movie! I began to realize that much of this stuff was just made up."

After seeing *The Craft*, Sarah started going back to church. Some of her friends and youth leaders at church have told her that Jesus is real, and she hopes to experience him. She looks forward to fun and interesting youth-group activities and lively worship rather than sitting in a pew week after week.

"The church has to realize that there are a lot of curious kids like me who won't accept the easy answers," she warns. "We need people willing to come alongside us as we look into things like Wicca, not to condemn us."

Sarah's words are worth heeding. Like Sarah, most Wiccans and Pagans have chosen their path after some serious thinking. In Sarah's case, her temporary involvement in Wicca was a backlash against America's shallow teenage culture, which isn't a bad reason to have such a reaction!

Like Sarah, some teenage girls are frustrated with the culture's overemphasis on body image and the pressure to be thin and look good. They like Wicca because it purports to revere women's bodies as sacred—mysteriously linked to the rhythms and cycles of nature.

We need not look any further than the explosive growth of plastic surgery to understand how our culture objectifies women. Women's bodies are often treated only as eye candy for men, and women are complicit in much of this. Many women and girls who embrace Wicca are rebelling against this trend.

According to studies conducted at Stanford University and the University of Massachusetts, nearly "70 percent of college women say they feel worse about their own looks after reading women's magazines."[2] Researchers at Brigham and Women's Hospital in Boston "found that the more frequently girls read magazines, the more likely they were to diet and to feel that magazines influence their ideal body shape. Nearly half reported wanting to lose weight because of a magazine picture (but only 29 percent were actually overweight)."[3]

Author and speaker Jean Kilbourne has monitored the advertising industry for years and believes it has had a great impact on modern culture, particularly on women. Her book *Deadly Persuasion: Why Women and Girls Must Fight the Addictive Power of Advertising* details thousands of examples in which advertisers subtly suggest that women must be thin and that happiness comes from buying more products, especially clothes and makeup. According to one psychologist, teenage girls spend more than 9 billion dollars annually on makeup and skin products alone to enhance their appearance.[4]

Kilbourne goes on to say that advertising often portrays young women as helpless by putting them in weak and compromising positions. In her book she refers to an ad for clothing that features a teenager in a seductive pose. The caption reads USED. This is the name of the clothing brand, but the ad implies that the woman has indeed been used—sexually.[5]

Kilbourne also states that "a television commercial for candy features a series of vignettes in which what a woman does for others (such as making a costume for her daughter) is ignored and unappreciated. At the end of each vignette, the woman pops a piece of candy in her mouth and says, 'I thank me very much with [Andes candies].'"[6] This ad sends the message that the way women cope with disappointment is to eat.

Amid this secular swirl, many young women see Wicca as a way to be grounded, to escape the deluge of cultural and media pressures that bombard them every day. Many Wiccans see themselves as living above this fray, which enables them to make some sort of difference in the world. And many are drawn to Wicca because they want to make a difference.

Consider what Ann Belford Ulanov, a Jungian psychologist, says about the word *witch:* "[The witch] stirs up storms that invade whole communities of people…. She enters [the community]. She changes it…. She heralds the timeless process originating out of the unconscious new forms of human consciousness and society."[7] The idea of the witch—powerful, magical, and controlling—resonates with many women as Wicca grows more popular.

But does the witch really stir up storms and change and invade civilized community? Or is this more of a projection of what Wiccan women hope to do? The desire for another type of spirituality runs deeper than the idea of a witch or the matriarchal myth. It reflects a desperate desire to be honored and noticed as women.

Something Greater Than Ourselves

Mary Daly would say that dignity comes from women themselves. But Mardi Keyes, the codirector of L'Abri Fellowship in Massachusetts, not too far down the road from Harvard, takes a different approach from Daly's. She says that women are liberated because of what God has done through Christ. Mardi also says that because Christianity has a transcendent Creator who is completely good and declares that injustices toward women such as rape and incest are wrong, we have grounds on which to condemn injustice. She argues that it is not enough to say that injustice against women goes against my own, or Mary Daly's, personal taste—that rape seems wrong to me or, in my opinion, denying a woman a job because she is a woman is bad. No, we need something greater, higher. Mardi argues that human dignity comes from being created in the image of God and is therefore shared by every human being, whatever a person's religious beliefs. Indeed, as she points out, "the only adequate basis we have to condemn injustice against anyone is ultimately the character of a transcendent Creator who is personal and holy and has revealed his moral will. This is true whether or not we have a relationship with God."

L'Abri was started in 1955 in Switzerland by American theologian Francis Schaeffer and his wife, Edith. Their goal was to open their home and have it be a place where people might find caring Christians who would offer satisfying answers to their questions. *L'abri* means "shelter" in French, a fitting name for their ministry, since the Schaeffers sought to provide a shelter from the pressures of our society. Since the original Swiss L'Abri began, other "shelters" have sprung up in several countries, including the one Mardi and her husband, Dick, direct outside of Boston.

A real pioneer in the area of fostering dialogue with feminists, Mardi travels around the country speaking on college campuses and engaging young women, which include neo-Pagan feminists, in thoughtful conversation about these issues. Christian campus groups usually ask her to speak, so the first thing she does is to urge a group to get the lecture jointly sponsored by a feminist or women's-studies group. She insists that the venue be neutral—not in a chapel or in the usual meeting place of either group. She also asks that the talk be an open lecture for everyone on campus, and she always allows time for discussion.

Reactions to this approach have been largely positive. Mardi starts her talks by admitting that the church doesn't have the best track record on women's issues. Taking ownership of the mistakes of the church—admitting that some professing Christians have been racist and sexist—immediately sets the tone for constructive dialogue. Her approach surprises those who come expecting a fight, and they become interested in hearing what she has to say.[8]

In today's world it is vital to encourage those listening to ask the bigger questions, such as, Who are we? Are we here by chance? Do we have dignity as human beings, and if so, where does it come from? So many people who have been turned off by the church get caught up in their personal experiences or in the political issues of the day and neglect to think seriously about these crucial issues. Taking a step back and asking the bigger questions allows for deeper discussion. It is also important to think seriously about the language Christians use and be in tune with the language feminists, Wiccans, and Pagans use. The apostle Paul used language familiar to his audience when he was defending the Christian faith on Mars Hill, so this is not new territory!

My friend Lilian, with the Damaris Project, likes to say that Christians would not send pastors or missionaries to China without instructing them in the language, customs, and culture of the Chinese people. Should Christians living in American culture be any different? Shouldn't we learn how to relate to those around us whose language, customs, and cultures differ from ours? Or are we to be like Mrs. Jellyby in Charles Dickens's *Bleak House,* whose philanthropic schemes consume her—the further away the cause, the better—even as people around her suffer? Or are we to be like Voltaire's Pangloss in *Candide,* who cared only about tending his own garden? We know in our hearts that Jesus wouldn't approve of either approach. Instead, he calls his followers to life on a deeper level where we might get our feet dirty and our egos deflated, but where life is much more real and exciting.

What Value Does Paganism Offer?

Paganism presents another dilemma: According to Paganism, human beings have the same value as rocks, trees, or animals. When British missionary William Carey went to India in the late eighteenth century, he lived among goddess-worshiping cultures in which widow burning was prevalent. When a woman's husband died, the widow would plunge to her death into the blazing funeral pyre of her husband. Because of the pantheistic worldview of the goddess-worshiping culture, the Indians saw nothing wrong with this—the woman was no more important than an inanimate object. This practice was eventually stopped due to the tireless efforts of Carey, who argued that women are made in God's image and therefore have dignity.

Carey also exerted his influence to stop infanticide by Goddess worshipers in India. Every winter, mothers pushed their babies down the mud banks into the river to either drown or be devoured by crocodiles. This was looked upon as a most holy sacrifice—giving the fruit of their wombs to Mother Ganges—the Goddess—in payment for the sins of their souls.

Jesus's Unusual Treatment of Women

Today Christianity is often regarded as the oppressor religion. It is true that many have used the name of Christ for nefarious purposes over the centuries. But in doing so they have strayed very far from the gospel's intent. In the Gospels Jesus interacted with women in ways that would seem normal today but were unheard of for first-century Palestine.

In the book of John, for example, we read that Jesus talked to a Samaritan woman at a well. (See John 4.) This was a radical interaction because Jews considered Samaritans outcasts at the time, and speaking with a woman would have been seen as beneath Jesus. When Jesus's disciples returned from town and found him talking to a Samaritan woman, Scripture says that even *they* were surprised.

In the book of Luke we read about a woman named Mary who sat at Jesus's feet listening to every word he said. But her sister, Martha, complained that Mary wasn't helping her in the kitchen. Jesus responded by gently scolding Martha for criticizing her sister and not choosing the better activity. (See Luke 10:38-42.) In the ancient world, women were not permitted to study under the rabbis, yet Jesus encouraged Mary and Martha to sit and learn from him.

Luke also tells us that Jesus was not intimidated by powerful women.

In Luke 8 we learn that Mary Magdalene and two other women, Joanna and Susanna, were among several women who actually bankrolled Jesus's ministry! Luke 8:3 says that these women were "helping to support [Jesus and the disciples] out of their own means."

Christian teaching and behavior ran counter to the ancient pagan culture of the Roman Empire. The Greek philosopher Aristotle, a prominent pagan, taught that a woman ranked somewhere between a man and a slave. Plato taught that if a man lived a cowardly life, he would be reincarnated as a woman. In his book about the early church, *The Rise of Christianity*, sociologist Rodney Stark writes that the Greco-Roman world was largely male due to female infanticide. By contrast, the early church was predominantly female. Female infanticide is a sign that women don't matter in society. Plato and Aristotle recommended infanticide as state policy, but Christians prohibited female infanticide, so Christianity was clearly countercultural in this respect. In Athens, women were usually forced to marry either before or at puberty, and they received little or no education. Husbands could divorce their wives by simply ordering them out of the household. By contrast, Christians condemned divorce, incest, marital infidelity, and polygamy. Female chastity was highly valued, as it was among pagans, but unlike pagans, Christians rejected the double standard that allowed men more sexual license than women. Christians believed that God commanded men to be chaste until marriage and to remain faithful to their wives once they married. Stark writes that Christian women enjoyed substantially higher status within the Christian subculture than pagan women did in the world at large.[9]

But we all know that the gospel message has been distorted over the years, and as a result, women have suffered. Jesus had high respect for women, but some early-church leaders did make some comments against women. Irenaeus, the bishop of Lyons who lived in the second century, said, "Both nature and the law place the woman in a subordinate condition to man." The early Roman theologian Tertullian, who also lived in the second century, said, "Woman destroyed so early, God's image, man."

Both of these statements contradict Scripture, which says that men and women are equal in God's eyes and that both man and woman are made in God's image. Fortunately, other early-church leaders got it right. Cyprian, the well-known third-century bishop of Carthage, said, "The mercy of Christ...was equally divided among everyone without difference of sex, years, persons."

As a woman, I can honestly say that a return to paganism does not seem very appealing or very progressive. What is clear is that while people will stumble, the gospel message does not: Jesus liberates women.

Strong Christian Women

Despite the best efforts of some men, strong Christian women managed to carve a place for themselves in history. The youngest in her family, Catherine of Siena lived during the second half of the fourteenth century and proved to be a mighty force in her day.

Over the protests of her family, she entered the Dominican order at age eighteen. At age twenty-one she began to serve the poor. According to her biographer, turmoil and political strife were rampant in Italy at the time, and whenever Catherine saw truth compromised, she was drawn to intercede. In her late twenties she began to intervene in antichurch activities. In a letter-writing campaign, she even persuaded English mercenaries to stop ravaging the Italian countryside. She founded a monastery at age thirty and devoted her life to peacemaking and preaching.

Catherine soon began to plead for peace between two cities at odds—Florence and Rome. She also lobbied against a papal schism in the church. She became so concerned over the church's troubles that she set up a household in Rome with male and female inhabitants who shared her cause and lived on alms.

Her great work, a beautiful orthodox vision of Christian spirituality called *The Dialogue,* was written over a two-year period when she was around thirty. She died at age thirty-three, having founded a monastery, been a diplomat, preached the Word of God, and written a book.[10]

Another strong and remarkable Christian woman was Teresa of Ávila, who was born in 1515 and, in the course of her lifetime, founded no less than seventeen convents across Spain. She combined contemplative religious life with a life of great activity. She also wrote several books. One of her most famous was *My Life,* which she was encouraged by her confessors to write. An honest and revealing book, *My Life* shows that there was no false piety in Teresa. The introduction to the Penguin Classics edition notes that Teresa admitted she would rather do more mindless tasks like spinning rather than write such a tome. It also notes that she confessed to being fond of the medieval equivalent of trashy romance novels, "romances of chivalry," and tells the reader that in her youth she sought to consort with bad company.[11]

These very real and strong women were wholly devoted to their faith and were used by God in mighty ways. They found their dignity in serving Christ and, thereby, serving the community around them. The constraints that medieval society placed on women did not hold them back.

EARLY FEMINISTS

What is interesting, however, and rarely discussed in feminist, Pagan, or Christian circles is the role Christianity played in the lives of some of the early feminists.

In 1848, the first women's-rights convention in the United States was held in Seneca Falls, New York, at the behest of a group of Quaker women. The two most prominent among them were Elizabeth Cady Stanton and Lucretia Mott. Many of the women in attendance were abolitionists who were also Christians, no doubt having been inspired by British parliamentarian William Wilberforce, whose Christian convictions led to his life's work of abolishing the British slave trade.

One woman at the convention was Sojourner Truth, a former slave who was inspired at Seneca Falls to advocate for women's rights. Sojourner had been freed from slavery when she was twenty-eight. She was also a Quaker and was compelled by Christian convictions. She knew that when men used the Bible as justification to treat women as second-class citizens, they were distorting its message.

A biography of Sojourner Truth states that in 1851 she attended a women's-rights convention in Akron, Ohio. She sat at the back and listened to several men make the case against women's rights. One man quoted a newspaper article that suggested "a woman's place is at home taking care of her children."

This comment surprised Sojourner because no one had ever given her the opportunity to stay home and take care of her children.

Her biographer wrote, "All morning she'd listened to preachers—men who ought to know better—use the Bible to support their own dead-end purposes. She was furious and ready to do battle using God's own truth."

After a while Sojourner spoke.

"That man over there...he says women need to be helped into carriages and lifted over ditches and to have the best everywhere. Nobody ever helps me into carriages, over mud puddles, or gets me to any best places.... And ain't I a woman?"

She continued as she turned to the men. " 'Look at me!' She bared her right arm and raised it in the air. The audience gasped as one voice. Her dark arm was muscular, made strong by hard work. 'I have ploughed. And I have planted.... And I have gathered into barns. And no man could head me.... And ain't I a woman?

'I have borne [thirteen] children and seen them sold into slavery, and when I cried out in a mother's grief, none heard me but Jesus. And ain't I a woman?...

'You say Jesus was a man so that means God favors men over women. Where did your Christ come from?... Man had nothing to do with him.' "[12]

Sojourner Truth knew that God gives special dignity to all human beings, male or female, slave or free. She was not motivated by an earlier myth of a peaceful matriarchy in which women were rulers. She also knew that the wives of slave owners were equally complicit in the plight of her people. She was motivated because she believed in what she knew to be bedrock truth: Because women are created in the image of God, they have special dignity as human beings.

Political Gains Were Not Enough

Another early feminist activist started out her crusade for women's rights as a secular activist. She thought that if women could only be put in charge of the world, things would turn out okay. Her name was Christabel Pankhurst. She lived in England and was agitating for women's rights in the United Kingdom several decades after Sojourner Truth.

Daughter of English suffrage activist Emmeline Pankhurst, Christabel came to Christian faith in 1918 shortly after women thirty years of age and older received the right to vote in Britain. Christabel and her mother, Emmeline, while perhaps less well known to the American reader, would be recognized by most British schoolchildren, just as Susan B. Anthony or Elizabeth Cady Stanton are recognized in the United States. I remember learning about the Pankhursts as a fourteen-year-old. What is often not discussed is the work Christabel did after British women got the right to vote.

The version of feminism that Christabel had always believed in came from her deep conviction of how society ought to be—marked by gender equality under the law. She carried this conviction all her life, but shortly after women got the vote, she realized that not even voting equality was enough to save society. Feminism was not enough to sustain her. World War I also shattered her idealistic view that humans could work toward progressive peace and prosperity. She came to realize that what was wrong with the world is inherent sin, and no amount of votes for women or striving on their part could bring about that peace she so longed for. Her writings provide us with a window into her mind: "We went forward with great trouble, to ourselves and to other people, to get votes for women. Well, we succeeded; but we find it is not enough, and we find that *we* are not enough!" She then gave this warning about what can hinder real progress toward peace and equality among all men and women: "If you place your ideals lower than Christ you will be disappointed."[13]

Christabel Pankhurst never gave up her feminist convictions; she just subsumed them as part of her Christianity. That might sound unusual to us, but I think she has it right. If Christians worship a God who is perfectly just and perfectly good, then equal dignity for women is something God wants. If Christians had been living the way God wanted them to all along, there would never have been a need for feminism at all, for women would have been equal in value to men.

Perhaps surprisingly, Christabel went on to be a best-selling evangelical author and a high-profile speaker on the fundamentalist circuit in the United States, of all places. Not only did she preach, but she shared the stage with people affiliated with theologically conservative colleges and universities.

Christabel's desire for progressive peace and prosperity reminds me of Margot Adler's call at the end of the Seattle conference for a religion that would mix feminism and ecology and help us get beyond wars and fighting. Adler's hope is typical of progressives—that with our modern knowledge and progress for women, we could rise above such events as the terrorist attacks of September 11. When Christabel wrote that votes for women were not enough, indeed that neither she nor her fellow agitators were enough, she realized that the only one to overcome the pain in this world is Jesus—in that one ritual he did for us on the cross two thousand years ago.[14]

LONGING FOR LIBERATION

Many women who embrace Wicca or Goddess spirituality long to be liberated from traditional female roles. Yet I believe that their neo-Pagan beliefs contain inherent contradictions. Knowing the history of Wicca, complete with Gardner's interest in nudism and Crowley's love for sex magic, I could not say that Wicca on its own merits seems to be liberating for women.

Some Goddess worshipers embrace traditional roles. They believe such roles give them power. As women they are the gender that gives life and birth. They don't seek to change their role or be liberated from it; rather, they revel in it and use it to get what they want. It is part of their power and the power of the Divine Feminine. But it is also limiting.

According to this view, the Goddess is a symbol of what women are expected to be. She embodies the best and worst of women's nature. While Aphrodite might represent our loving side, Athena represents the warrior within, the mean and vindictive part of our human nature. The question is, do we really want the divine to be subject to our flaws and shortcomings? Because God is beyond gender and human limits, God allows both men and women to transcend traditional feminine or masculine traits and become whole people regardless of race, background, or sex. What Christians know that is different from what Goddess worshipers believe is that *they can't become those whole people by themselves.* Left to their own devices, they will reduce spirituality to fit their own categories, often with less-than-desirable results. But the power of the Holy Spirit enables them to change.

I believe that without knowing it, the gospel message is what Margot Adler longed for as she clutched the microphone in Seattle. After all her striving for votes for women and a peaceful society, the gospel is what Christabel Pankhurst found to be true.

And the yearning starts young, as we'll see in the next chapter.

"It's Malleable"

Wicca and Teens

H ail Fair Moon, ruler of the night, guard me and mine until the light. Hail Fair Sun, ruler of the day, make the morn light my way," Jess chanted in front of lighted candles on a small altar in the corner of her bedroom. This altar is also where Jess casts spells and performs rituals.

Jess, a student at a Washington private school where her classmates are the sons and daughters of the power elite, had on her altar four porcelain chalices that represented the elements of air, water, fire, and earth. In each chalice she had placed rose petals, semiprecious stones, melted candle wax, and dried leaves. Each chalice rested on a corner of a five-pointed star, the pentagram. Jess placed a frog on the fifth point, which she says represents spirit or life.

I asked Jess if the spells work.

"Sure," she giggled. "Too well, sometimes!" She then told me about a spell she cast to keep a boy away from a friend. She admitted to feeling frightened at times while practicing witchcraft and confessed that she even stopped for a while, but the appeal of Wicca overcame her hesitations.

"Wicca allows me to create my own religion, and that suits me. It's malleable," Jess told me as we sat outside a coffee shop across the street from her school. Like most of the teenagers I spoke with, Jess likes Wicca because she can adapt it to meet her needs. Also, like many teens, Jess admitted that she was looking to fill a spiritual void in her life. She had been raised by secular Jewish parents, and she longed for some sort of spirituality of her own. She found Wicca on the Internet. "I needed to believe in something," she said as she looked wistfully at the gray autumn sky. "Everyone needs something to latch on to."

TEENS EMBRACE WICCA

Jess is one of a growing number of young people who are interested in Wicca and Pagan practices. Sixteen-year-old Alice from Northern Virginia told me that she is intrigued by the feminine Goddess of Wicca and has decided that other religions have nothing in them for women. She practices witchcraft alone, preferring not to divulge the privacy of her rituals to anyone. Her mother does not enter her room, Alice says, honoring her request to keep all negative energy outside of her space. Both Jess and Alice insisted that they feel empowered by Wicca and cast spells to evoke change in their lives and in the lives of others.

Conduct the following survey and consider the results; they might surprise you. Five years ago they surprised me. Find a group of seventeen-year-old girls in private or public schools, in red states or blue, and ask if any of them have Wiccan friends or know people interested in Wicca. When I asked a group of teenagers at my church this question, all the girls raised their hands. At that point I knew that Wicca was moving into mainstream culture.

The interest in Wicca among teens is not confined, as one might think, to big cities such as Washington, DC, or New York. I met seventeen-year-old Ellen and her friend Deana, whom I mentioned at the beginning of the book, at a bookstore in suburban Charlotte, North Carolina. They told me how they had become practicing Wiccans. There was nothing unusual about their appearance. Ellen had long blond hair, wore a bright yellow My

Little Pony T-shirt underneath a gray warmup suit, and had a Wiccan pentagram around her neck. Deana was dressed similarly in jeans and a T-shirt. As she talked she fiddled with a necklace of the goddess Diana.

Neither Deana nor Ellen was aware of the origins of modern Wicca. Both had heard of Gerald Gardner and knew that he promoted a branch of Wicca called Gardnerian Wicca, but they had only a vague notion of how he appropriated and invented many of the rituals used today. Neither of the girls knew anything about Aleister Crowley, nor did they seem to care. As with most Wiccans, it was the experience that mattered to them—how they felt when they practiced rituals.

WHAT DRAWS THEM?

The generation born in the 1980s and 1990s is frequently referred to as the Millennials. William Strauss and Neil Howe, authors of the book *Generations,* write that the Millennials are less violent, vulgar, and sexually charged than the teen culture that adults are producing for them. They are serious about their spirituality and its rituals but prefer to structure its tenets to suit their needs. George Barna refers to this generation as the Mosaics because of their eclectic spiritual interests and lifestyle, "their nonlinear thinking style, the fluidity of their personal relationships, [and] their cut-and-paste values profile."[1]

A recent Gallup poll confirms this: While 84 percent of the teenagers surveyed reported that religion is important to them, many of those teens said that they are more "spiritual" than religious and participate in less orthodox practices. Teens are seeking spiritual experiences but want to define those experiences in their own terms.

So young people like the fact that Wicca can be blended with other faiths. Wicca gives them permission to create a religion that lacks any sort of abstract moral judgment other than that of their own design or choosing. They view Wicca as a positive and life-affirming religion, passive and nonviolent.

Young people who practice Wicca are usually dissatisfied with their own spiritual experience in some way. They might feel forced to go to church, though they don't believe in the gospel. They may have been raised without a religion, and they long for something more than what our secular culture has to offer. Others lead such unstructured lives that they long for some sort of ritual, something they can control. And, of course, the paranormal has always fascinated young people—they have a curiosity about the unknown. For some teenagers, practicing Wicca is a form of rebellion, but I found that the majority of young people were very intelligent and thoughtful about their spiritual choices.

In fact, I discovered in my research that teens apathetic about religion in general were not the ones drawn to Wicca. Most of the Wiccan teens seemed to harbor deep feelings of resentment toward the church. Many complained about peers who embraced a faith without understanding or challenging its doctrines. Girls liked the idea that, as a belief system, Wicca is somewhat complicated and mysterious. What I soon realized was that they are willing to reject other equally complicated and mysterious faiths in favor of Wicca because Wicca has no orthodoxy: They could simply add or subtract elements of it at random.

While some teens remain content to dabble in occult magical practices, such as reading tarot cards or casting love spells, others are more serious about their practice. Most teenagers practice Wicca alone, but as they get older, they might join covens. In some covens drug use is the norm, although others reject substance abuse altogether. Most teens I spoke with said they wouldn't use drugs in rituals, but a few insisted that drugs are necessary. *The Pagan Census,* comprised of a ten-year study of neo-Pagans by sociologist Helen Berger, found that of those surveyed, a slight majority of neo-Pagans believe that the use of mind-altering substances is a valid magical practice.[2] There is no way to tell how many teens agree with that because those who do use illegal substances would not admit to using them if asked.

Although we can't track the exact numbers of teens who practice Wicca, it is not difficult to observe the trend in the culture at large. Fritz Jung, the creator of The Witches' Voice Web site, told me that teenagers who practice Wicca alone or who meet in small informal groups are the hardest to track. What Jung does know is that 35 percent of the total visitors to The Witches' Voice are under eighteen. The Witches' Voice Web page for teenagers—"So You Wanna Be a Witch"—drew 175,000 visitors over a two-year period.

Spin magazine, in its "Grrrl Power" issue in 2000, placed witchcraft at the top of the list of interests among teenage girls.[3] *Jump* magazine, a monthly magazine for teenage girls, featured a fashion article on "goddess style." The magazine's editor noted that *Jump* refrains from directly referring to witchcraft but fills "its pages with features on astrology, herbal cures and color therapy"—witches' paraphernalia.[4]

Beliefnet.com is the largest religion and spirituality Web site on the Internet. Since its launch in 1999, Beliefnet has included a section called Earth-Based Spirituality, which includes Wicca. Beliefnet's religion producer told me that they knew it was becoming more popular, but they were unsure how much prominence to give it on the site. Over the years earth-based spirituality has become the second most popular form of spirituality on the site, after Christianity. Occasionally earth-based spirituality slips into third place behind Buddhism, and the Islam section had much more traffic after September 11, but earth-based spirituality has stayed near the top of the list. Much of the traffic on the earth-based site is generated by teenagers, and most of the discussion centers around Wicca.

"The contemporary witch is the beautiful 25 year old that you see on TV," Llewellyn publicist Jami Shoemaker told the *New York Times*.[5] The contemporary witch is also the fifteen-year-old girl who found Wicca on bookstore shelves and the seventeen-year-old boy who was fed up with cultural Christianity and did not want to embrace the religion of his parents. The contemporary witch, in reality, is a young person at a highly impressionable age, just beginning to think for herself, strongly influenced by her peers, and ready to experience something she sees as original, real, and as unrestricting as she wants to make it.

FEELING EMPOWERED

Deana and Ellen's practice of Wicca is typical of their generation—a mix of many things they have read in books or seen on the Internet. Because Deana's parents do not know she is Wiccan, she keeps no books about Wicca in her house but borrows books from Ellen and also attends rituals with Ellen.

Ellen was raised without any faith. Her parents had been Jehovah's Witnesses but rejected these beliefs after they got married. They decided not to go to church because they were turned off by what they felt was the hypocrisy of Southern Baptists in their community. But the numbers of Wiccans and neo-Pagans in Charlotte is growing—even in a city with a highway named after evangelist Billy Graham! Ellen told me she dislikes the commercialization of Christmas, particularly, and both girls feel that many Christians are hypocrites. What they dislike is not the message of Christ himself but many of the people who purport to be his followers.

Like Deana, Ellen became interested in Wicca by reading a book by Raymond Buckland. Soon after she read this book, she saw the movie *The Craft*, which piqued her interest even more.

"After watching that movie and the girls who cast spells and become powerful, I think many girls were like, 'Wow! Cool!'" Ellen told me. "I wonder if I can do those things too!"

Ellen admitted to drug use and mentioned that her parents let her smoke pot. "It just makes rituals a lot better," she insisted. Deana agreed.

"Ellen's parents are an exception, though," Deana noted. "They are really liberal. A few years ago you couldn't find anyone who knew anything about Wicca. Today—just look around you! Young people are leading the way; they know way more about this stuff than their parents."

On the sales rack behind her was a set of greeting cards with "Send a Note, Cast a Spell" printed in soft colors.

"See!" Deana said as she opened the packet to investigate its authenticity. "We don't even have to move from our seats to find Wiccan things now!"

Each card had a different spell on the back—spells to mend a broken heart, spark passion, reignite love, or kindle romance. Both girls nodded approvingly at the cards.

"These are good. They are a little silly, but if people read these, they will soon be led to better things to read," said Ellen. Both Deana and Ellen told me that they are utterly amazed at the way Wicca has been marketed in recent years.

"Five years ago you couldn't find books about Wicca or spells in large bookstores, but it would be easy to get interested in Wicca now," Deana said as she waved her arm in the direction of the bookshelves.

"After I read the book about love spells, what really began to attract me was that Wicca respects nature, that god is in nature, that Wicca focuses on protecting the environment, and that it empowers women," Deana told me.

It can be difficult for impressionable teens to know where fact ends and fiction begins. Publishers of Wicca books repeatedly insisted that they view these Wicca books as sheer fantasy and fun. As I mentioned previously, this is not, however, what older neo-Pagans think. Wicca is spiritually real, and kids are tapping into unseen supernatural forces when they practice it.

"Wicca lets you be really creative at the holidays," Ellen told me breezily as she passed her coffee to Deana. In December, at Ellen's house, they celebrated the pagan holiday of Yule rather than Christmas. "I found some cool rituals on the Internet," said Ellen. "We had a great dinner with my parents." Deana still celebrated Christmas at her house with her parents.

Ellen had given Deana the goddess necklace that hung around her neck as a Yule gift. Deana clutched the pendant in her right hand as she talked. "A lot of girls like the idea that they can be powerful if they practice Wicca. But part of me hesitates to become a full-fledged Wiccan because I would hate for my kids to miss out on Christmas. My child would be the poor Wiccan kid who has to celebrate something else. I'd like to celebrate both."

Ellen shook her head, her jaw firm. "No! I won't do that. I have rejected Christianity to be a full-fledged Pagan. Yule will be celebrated in our house."

I asked Ellen and Deana where the power comes from. Can magic ever be harmful or scary?

Their answer was typical of many Wiccans I encountered: They believe that Wicca can be harmful and that it can tap into some form of power, so individual practitioners must be careful not to use Wicca to harm others. In sum, Wiccans don't fear that those "powers" will ever be able to control them. In their spiritual worldview, humans are the arbiters of both physical and spiritual power. Ultimate good does not win out in the end because, according to Wiccans, there is no such thing as ultimate good. All power resides with the individual practitioner. Both Deana and Ellen say that Wicca makes them feel empowered, and this is why they like it.

THE NEED TO BELIEVE IN SOMETHING REAL

"Wicca is not all nice and safe," Laura whispered to me with a tremor in her voice as her classmates joked and bantered. She looked at me tentatively and lowered her voice. "I can't sleep without the light on anymore! I am haunted by a scary presence at night. People think I'm odd, but something happened!"

Laura, a practicing Wiccan, told me that one night she and two girl-friends were preparing for a meditation. "We were trying to channel energy through one of my friends to knock down a mental wall, and we felt a flut-ter of unprotected power," she whispered. "We didn't know what we were doing and felt like there was a presence watching us, so we fled the house. My friend heard voices. We went to a park, and it came near us. We had a very bad experience. One of my friends does not believe anymore at all. You cannot mention spirituality to her. My other friend started having problems with voices and visions. She practices but is very scared. If I think about it, I cry."

I asked her why she still practiced Wicca if it had scared her so badly. She said she had not properly shielded herself from "unwanted" spirits but was learning to do that now from an older, more experienced Wiccan who had also had a similar experience when she was young. Laura is determined to continue.

"I kept telling myself I have to believe! Oh, I really have to believe," she said breathlessly. "This is real to me, and I want to practice it correctly."

Laura was raised by a Catholic father and a mother whom she labels agnostic Methodist. But Laura says that Catholicism was never real to her father, and he never convinced her of its worthiness. Like Ellen, she went to see *The Craft*. At first Laura thought the movie was silly. She and her friends had gathered for a weekend party and were having fun mocking the film. Most already practiced other religions and had no interest in *The Craft*. But Laura was more than intrigued. That week she read a book about a tradition called fairy Wicca and began to experiment.

Along with her boyfriend, Scott, Laura is a member of a Pagan club at a high school in rural northern California. The club is officially sanctioned by the school and has its own teacher-supervisor. Some of the students' parents are also involved.

Scott's mother has been interested in Wicca for years, although she still takes him to a local Lutheran church on occasion. He became interested in neo-Paganism after he was almost struck by lightning. He discovered that the ancient Norse and Celtic peoples had gods and goddesses related to the weather and that the Norse god of thunder is Thor. Thor is also known as the god of the common man and the working man, which resonated with Scott because he likes to help people.

Scott grew up going to a Lutheran church, attended Sunday school, and was an acolyte during church services. He studied the Scriptures and subsequently had many questions. He told me that the answers his pastor gave him never seemed to fully address his questions, and he grew frustrated.

"Wicca, on the other hand, is empowering. It makes you feel part of something, and it doesn't care who or what you are. You could be born male and feel very female, and it doesn't care. It is a religion that is very unbiased. I think that is what draws a lot of people toward it. It is a very tolerant religion. As long as you are willing to accept the consequences of your actions—that what you do will come back to you threefold, with karma."

I met Jack, a junior in the club, and he told me that the only sure thing within the Craft is nature, the great Mother Goddess. It is something he can see, touch, and smell—it's real. It was almost as if he trusted nature over anything else.

"Nature is very loving to its creatures," he said, "but also very karmic." Jack wore a necklace with an Egyptian ankh around his neck, a symbol used in ancient Egypt to represent eternal life.

Jack came to the meeting with his mother, Kate. She came because it was her day off, and she had discovered Wicca the same time her son did. I asked Kate what drew her to Wicca and what encouraged her to support her son in his Wiccan beliefs. After she thought about it a moment, she answered, "It is very oriented toward women. You become empowered by all these things. It was like opening a box—Pandora's box of very cool things. It's a lot more interesting than what society says it is. Wicca has good intentions—you do nothing to harm others. The Bible is a list of don'ts!"

Kate said she loves to use the word *witch* to describe herself. "It is very mystical and magical. I identify with it as a woman."

Kate and all the members of the club agreed that Wicca is very popular among teenagers today. One reason, said Scott, is that there isn't much hierarchical leadership within Wicca. They also agreed that the items they use during worship are very important to them, almost sacred.

"This book took me two months to find," Laura told me as she pointed to a book on the Hindu goddess Kali, whom she had chosen as her personal goddess. "It is very precious to me—as are my tarot cards."

"Kali is the mother, but she is also known as the destroyer," Laura told me. In fact, in India, animals are sacrificed every day to assuage Kali's thirst for blood. Laura bought her tarot cards at a neo-Pagan festival she had recently attended with Scott. The pair were amazed by the number of people attending the festival. Scott attended a lecture on Norse spirituality, which he described as somewhat shallow. Both were a little shocked at a booth dealing with ritual sex, where whips and chains were for sale.

"Yeah. I steered clear of that one," Scott joked, laughing rather nervously.

Sonya, a seventeen-year-old club member, is sympathetic to Wicca but doesn't call herself Wiccan. She told me she is a "kitchen witch" instead.

"I'm less into the rituals and spells but more into the healing properties of the herbs that Wiccans use in their spells," she explained. "I prefer to adopt the tenets of Wicca—its respect for nature and how it empowers women—rather than fully practice it."

Sonya is typical of many teenagers today. While some practice Wicca very seriously, others are less committed, preferring to pick and choose the parts of the religion that suit them best. Sonya told me that she's interested in health issues, so the focus on herbal healing in Wiccan spells appeals to her.

The current renewed interest in organic products and alternative medicine mushroomed in popularity about the same time Wicca did. As our culture becomes increasingly post-Christian but more spiritual, it is not difficult to see how someone like Sonya can use Wicca to make a religion out of an alternative lifestyle. For the past forty years, our culture has glorified fast food and the convenience of TV dinners and prepackaged products. Childhood obesity has skyrocketed, and type 2 diabetes is at unprecedented levels. Many health-conscious Millennials/Mosaics would not find anything unusual about Sonya's being a "kitchen witch" in our current toxic environment. They have, after all, been characterized as a sensible, efficient generation that uses nonlinear approaches to religion—a perfect combination for vulnerability to a flexible spirituality.

THE GLORIFICATION OF SELF

On the other side of the country, not too far from Salem at a Catholic prep school for girls in central Massachusetts, senior girls are taught about the Goddess traditions in their religion class.

The school is set on a leafy, thirteen-acre campus, formerly a private estate, and is run by a group of nuns. Most of the girls who attend are diligent in their studies and go to college upon graduation. Before they graduate, they are required to take a World Religions class in which they study such religions as Buddhism, Islam, and Judaism, and they also do a unit called The Goddess Traditions. Some of the class discussion focuses specifically on Wicca.

I spent a day interviewing students and attending classes with them. I learned that the World Religions curriculum was already in place when the current teacher was hired. She taught the material in a balanced and fair manner and told me that at the end of last year, an overwhelming majority of her students reported that of all the religions they studied during the course of the year, the Goddess unit had been the most meaningful to them. I was curious to know what about this topic intrigued these young women more than Buddhism or Islam did. But even more intriguing to me was whether or not some of the girls found the Goddess traditions more attractive than their own Catholicism.

As the seniors shuffled in to their World Religions class, I noticed that most fit the typical teenage profiles. There were the athletes, girls who wore Adidas flip-flops and thick, white tube socks. There were the preppier kids dressed crisply in J.Crew. The more artsy kids wore flowing skirts and jewelry. The class had just completed the Goddess unit, and their last homework assignment was to create their own goddess, incorporating the things they had learned about Goddess worship from class. Some had used construction paper, photos, and headlines from magazines, while others had simply drawn their own goddess using colored pens and pencils.

We sat in a circle, and one by one each student presented her goddess. The first student, clad in tracksuit pants, had created a warrior goddess—a woman dressed in army fatigues.

"Mine is a creator goddess," said another student named Erin, whose straight wheat-colored hair hung just beneath her chin. She wore a long khaki skirt, a pale pink T-shirt, and sensible low-heeled shoes as she pointed to a woman hovering over a picture of the earth. "She is all sexy and stuff. She is like a fertility goddess. She was there when the world was created; she is very earthy and powerful."

Next, a more historical perspective yielded the goddess Anna.

"She is not really the goddess of anything," said her creator, Sue, a small, pale, yet confident kid. "She was flirting with mortals. Zeus punished her and took away her voice."

A tall, blond girl named Tanya introduced Eve.

"This is Eve; she is the first woman. God created man and woman equal. She made the sky. She is also the crone; she is wise and a grandmother figure."

The similarities between the goddesses created by the girls and their own personalities were startling.

"How many of you were consciously putting yourself in your goddess?" asked their teacher with a smile. Some of the young girls gasped and cupped their hands over their mouths as they realized what they had done.

"She's everything I want to be," said Tanya. "I want to be equal with men but be a powerful and wise woman when I am older."

The athlete laughed self-consciously as she gazed at her warrior goddess dressed in army fatigues—her classmates nodded knowingly as they laughed with her.

In another class, one of the girls showed keen insight into Goddess worship and the spirituality of ancient pagan cultures. She simply pasted a mirror onto a piece of paper. Her reflection in the mirror was her goddess—herself. She understood that ancient pagan Goddess worship is ultimately a glorification of the self, as is much of modern Goddess worship.

"Debbie's understanding gets at the very heart of our unit," said the teacher, referring to their recent studies of the Goddess traditions and feminist spiritual liturgy. "Feminist liturgy seeks to help women recognize the power within," she explained.

One of the main complaints that Goddess worshipers have about the Christian church is that it is patriarchal. Some of the students in the classroom agreed.

"The Catholic church is entirely run by men; it is very patriarchal. I don't like the idea of women being banned from the priesthood," complained one student. Since Wiccans worship the Goddess, the students had discussed Wicca in their class. "I would never practice Wicca myself, but I think it is cool that women can be priestesses in Wicca."

The tone was different during the afternoon class. The students' goddess projects similarly resembled their own personalities, and they laughed when they, too, realized what they had done. But some girls were serious about their Catholic faith and less sympathetic to Goddess worship and Wicca.

One of the students, Mary, was dressed in black, had short, dark hair, wore glasses, and sat very quietly as her classmates discussed these issues animatedly. Soon one of her peers pointed at her and told me that she was a practicing Wiccan and that perhaps she could explain her choice of belief. Mary told us that a friend introduced her to Wicca. Her parents were Catholic, but their faith had left her unfulfilled.

"I didn't have any friends in the eighth grade anyway, except for one girl," said the seventeen-year-old senior. "She introduced me to Wicca, and I have been practicing ever since."

Mary's friend abandoned the practice, but Mary said she found something beautiful in Wicca and liked its respect for nature and its lack of rules, which she contrasted with her experience in the Catholic Church. Her peers, she told us, were surprisingly interested to hear about her spirituality. They, too, were fed up with the church and wanted to explore different faiths, although only Mary had actually done so. As she talked she played with a necklace of the Goddess that hung around her neck.

Mary lives in a small town and told us about the difficulty she had finding others who practice Wicca. "I found a few shops listed on the Internet and went looking for them one day but wasn't successful," she sighed. "So I am really grateful for the Internet where I can communicate with others who are Wiccan as well."

Mary's story is typical of many who are introduced to the world of Wicca simply through a friend, a book, a movie, or a Web site. As I left the school, I recalled that the teacher had told me this unit had been the most meaningful to the girls. They were typical teenagers longing to be noticed and honored for who they are as women. Again, the thought entered my mind: *A young and bright woman in America might ask herself, Why not Wicca?*

What Is a Parent to Do?

Except in rare cases like Ellen's or Jack's, most parents are not at all tolerant of their teenager's neo-Pagan interests, so most teenagers refrain from telling their parents about Wicca. But Christian parents, in particular, have good reason to be concerned about this. Christian parents who, like the Wiccan parents I met, understand and believe in a spirit world know very well what their children could be dealing with if left to their own devices. No Wiccan I have met has ever told me, when pressed, that Wicca was safe and free from negative spiritual consequences. Those parents who don't believe that Wicca is spiritually real are misguided. But is an alarmed response the best approach when dealing with a child who has become a Wiccan or is interested in exploring it further?

After talking to countless young people, I have concluded that the best approach for parents or concerned teachers is to first listen to their children and find out what interests them about Wicca. What do they like about it? What does it seem to offer that the Christian church doesn't offer? I think it is also important to become familiar with what young people are reading and learning about Wicca. As evidenced by Laura clutching her tarot cards and Deana prizing her necklace of the goddess Diana, most kids have a deep respect for their Wiccan "things"—books, mini-altars, spell kits, whatever. Don't assume you know what they all mean. Read about them and find out.

It's important for parents to be able to give an articulate response about why they believe what they do and why they believe it provides meaning. It is usually not enough to ban Wiccan activity and force a child or teenager to attend church. It may appear that the interest in Wicca has gone away, but it usually has not. If a young person is interested in Wicca, that interest likely developed over time and for a reason. It is important to discover that reason. Build on her intellectual curiosity and challenge her to think equally hard about Christian doctrine and what it really means. If you are also unsure about the meaning of Christian doctrine, you, too, might need to examine what you believe. Consult a pastor or someone who can answer your questions and those of your child. Or you might want to tap into resources available through L'Abri and other Christian organizations or read some books on Christianity. (See the resources section for some suggestions.) Otherwise, you will only frustrate your child.

Mary said as much as she and I continued our dialogue via e-mail after I left her school. She told me she was frustrated about not being able to go to Salem on Halloween and feels that her parents don't take time to understand what she believes.

"So here we are on Samhain, perhaps the biggest Wiccan holiday, and I can't do a thing. I want to go to Salem tonight with my boyfriend and his friends, but my mother has put her foot down. I can't wait until I can openly practice."

As we will see in the next chapter, that is exactly what happens when many students get to college.

Seeking Authentic Spirituality

Wicca and College Students

My parents have a strong ethic for going to church every week, but they don't really have a reason why," twenty-one-year-old Cathleen told me as I met with her college neo-Pagan club at a campus in Delaware. "I get the feeling they are following their faith blindly. I was never that way, but I got dragged to church until I graduated from high school, which stunk big time."

When she got to college, Cathleen told me, she was finally free of the constraints of her parents and could practice whatever religion she wanted. She is a wildlife-conservation major and first practiced Wicca because of its focus on nature and her perception that it elevates women. Now she practices a mix of Wicca and Native American spirituality. I asked Cathleen if she would have likely embraced Christianity had her parents' religious practices been more heartfelt rather than just based on tradition. After thinking about it for a moment, she nodded. "Probably."

Cathleen is one of many neo-Pagans on college campuses today. Many college students, like the high-school students I interviewed, prefer a DIY (Do It Yourself) religion. This allows them to tailor their spirituality to themselves rather than the other way around. What matters most is not whether their spirituality could be of universal help to others but that it works for them. Instead of being convinced or persuaded of a virtuous idea, model, or worldview, those who happen upon neo-Paganism tend to mold it to fit what they already believe. This struck me as something all young people might like to do. Rules are a pain and morals are a drag—why not jettison them for your own set? After all, college is the first opportunity most students get to do this sort of thing. Away from home for the first time, they are no longer under the watchful parental eye.

A NEW ATTRACTION

Since feminists first embraced it in the 1970s, Wicca has made inroads in the academic community. At the beginning Wicca gained popularity largely through women's studies departments, but now Wiccan covens and neo-Pagan groups, as well as classes, are flourishing on campuses nationwide.

Often neo-Pagan clubs receive money from student governments. The existence of such groups would have been unheard of as recently as thirty, twenty, ten, or five years ago, depending on the area of the country where you attended college. Harvard University's Pluralism Project Web site has links to more than one hundred recognized neo-Pagan student groups on college campuses nationwide. In almost every state, a Wiccan student can find a group of like-minded neo-Pagans with whom to bond during his or her student years.

The trend has been documented in the media. In 2000 the *Boston Globe* reported that "back to nature paganism" was growing in popularity on college campuses. Reporting that there were at least seven Pagan student groups in Massachusetts alone, the *Globe* discovered that students were drawn to neo-Paganism "as a spiritual offshoot of the emerging counter-culture of greens and antiglobalists."[1]

"It's natural for college students to be attracted to things they haven't thought or experienced before," University of California at Santa Barbara religion professor Christine Thomas told the *Globe*. "But this movement is a reflection of a lot of things: fascination with the occult, the lack of one religion's hegemony, and the explosion of information and networking opportunities available on the Internet."[2]

Several students told me that they decided to embrace Wicca or neo-Paganism in general because they want a spirituality that integrates itself into every aspect of their lives. They don't want a religion just for Sunday—something to do out of obligation or fear of going to hell. Like Cathleen, this is what they had seen their parents do. They want something authentic.

LOOKING FOR A HOLISTIC SPIRITUALITY

At a university in Pennsylvania, Wiccan students can be excused from class on their holidays. A glance at the university accommodation policy reveals that Wiccan holidays are listed along with the others, such as Christmas or Yom Kippur. According to the university's official documents, the policy "acknowledges the right of those who live and work and study [at the university] to engage in religious observances, and the University is pledged to honor the exercise of that right."[3]

When I contacted the student Pagan organization at the college, the president, Daniel, told me that his group was "on the rocks for membership." A practicing witch for five years, he told me that when he took over the group, although it had been in existence for five years at that point, the former president left him neither a list of interested Pagans on campus nor a list of alumni Pagans. As a result, he had to start from scratch. He perceived that many students on campus separated religious and academic life: Religion was for the weekends and not applicable to daily life. His efforts to integrate the two with this club were met with indifference. He also indicated that more and more Pagans his age were interested in practicing the

Craft by themselves—to create their own versions of Wicca or Paganism from what they read in books.

When the Pagan club was an active group, they discussed topics like divination and how they could integrate religion into their lives. Daniel told me that the need to integrate religion into his daily life is what propelled his interest in witchcraft. He had been raised in a Jewish home, and after his Bar Mitzvah at age thirteen, he was asked to read the Torah in Hebrew in front of the congregation. At this point, he'd had five years of Hebrew school and was looking forward to this experience. He practiced for a long time. As a language, Hebrew does not contain vowels, but his practice version of the Torah did. No one told him that the Torah in the synagogue would not contain the vowels he had grown used to reading. When the big day arrived, Daniel approached the Torah and was utterly unprepared to read the version without vowels. He choked and ended up in tears in front of the congregation.

"While I was mortified, this wasn't enough to cause me to break from Judaism, the religion I was raised with," he told me. It was the reaction of the congregants that turned him off.

During a lunch after the service, an older female member of the synagogue approached Daniel and told him that he had just experienced an AFLE, Another F****** Life Moment, and not to worry about it. Instead of feeling comforted, Daniel was shocked not only by her language but also by the fact that she did not seem to care that he had trained in Hebrew school for five years for this moment.

"I think the nonchalance that she had toward this is what made me realize that some within the congregation did not view their religion as seriously as I wanted to. I began to feel that you could leave your religion behind when you left the synagogue after the Sabbath and pick it up next week."

This was very disturbing to Daniel as an earnest thirteen-year-old, and he spent his remaining teenage years searching for a religion that would be a part of every aspect of his life. After learning about Buddhism, Christianity, and Scientology, he settled into a form of agnosticism but developed his own "mishmash of reincarnation, karma, and helping others." Daniel said that he rejected Christianity for some of the same reasons he rejected Judaism. Most of his friends who professed to be Christians also saw their faith as something reserved for Sundays. Daniel had always felt drawn to animism, so his own form of agnosticism resembled modern witchcraft. After a friend introduced him to Wicca, he read *Wicca: A Guide for the Solitary Practitioner* by Scott Cunningham, and five years later he is still practicing.

"Gods and Goddesses at Work in My Life"

Across the Delaware River, a Pagan club also thrives on a New Jersey college campus. Meg, the president, is a junior history-and-religion double major. She hopes to go to graduate school in religion and teach Paganism at the college level. Raised by a strict Roman Catholic mother, Meg attended church regularly as a child. But soon she grew weary of the doctrine of sin, the rules, and people telling you what to do. In high school she, like Daniel, could not understand the people who thought they were religious because they regularly attended church but whose faith had no impact on their lives.

"To me, being religious is being in touch, in personal relationship with your deity. If you are going to go through the ritual every week, you should care about your deity and what it means to worship in your daily life," she told me.

Meg became involved in a coven with some of her high-school friends, mainly from the drama club. Now she calls herself a solitary Pagan—she practices alone and keeps an altar to her major goddess in her bedroom.

"I don't want to sound freaky, but I remember my gods and goddesses throughout the day, and I get inspiration from them. I know they are at work in my life," she said.

I asked what her parents thought of her rejection of Catholicism.

"My dad doesn't really care, but my mom was upset about it for a while, and now it's just a taboo topic," she said wistfully. "I wish I could talk to my mom about it more."

Dorm-Room Pagan

On a campus in Ohio, fliers for the Pagan Student Association, or PSA, are often torn down by other students, and members of the PSA are sometimes told that they are going to hell. "But we're used to that," PSA's cochair, Mike, told me. Wicca and neo-Paganism are well known on campus but not yet accepted. A twenty-three-year-old continuing-education student, Mike has been a member of the group since he was eighteen. PSA even has one forty-six-year-old, but most members are eighteen or nineteen. When I contacted Mike, the group had been in existence for six years. At a weekly meeting they may have ten to twenty attendees, but they have had more than four hundred students attend their meetings over the years—some who were practicing Pagans and others who were just curious.

The group appeared to be fairly organized. Their meetings are usually workshops, lectures, or discussions. They also go camping and have pizza nights and parties. They attend local neo-Pagan festivals, but because there are so many different types of spiritualities in the group, they don't hold rituals themselves unless the rituals are part of a particular workshop. Meeting discussions have included such topics as amulets and talismans, the history of neo-Paganism, kitchen witchery, Egyptian magic, tarot-card readings, and herbalism.

One well-attended meeting is called Dorm-Room Pagan. This usually attracts interested freshmen, some of whom stay and others who do not. The session on herbalism is also popular because students like to learn how to make potpourri and teas. Some students are under the tutelage of more learned teachers of the Craft who teach classes based on their pagan traditions.

The spiritual makeup of the group is very eclectic. Mike himself is a Druid. Historically, Druids were members of Celtic religious orders of priests, soothsayers, judges, and poets in ancient Britain and Ireland. Modern-day Druids claim to engage in the same practices and beliefs as those ancient ones. The group also includes one Satanist, Mike told me. Most of the students in the group would disavow any link to Satanism, however, and most are not hostile to Christianity—they simply have no interest in practicing it. When Students for Free Thought wanted the PSA to help them get rid of prayer at graduation, the PSA declined because members couldn't decide if prayer was good or bad. Mike said he lost his own faith in Christianity during a time of crisis in his life as he wrestled with the age-old question of why there was evil in the world.

"I didn't believe that a just god or an omnipotent god would allow the existence of a devil or evil, so I simply disbelieved both. From there it was a short step away from Christianity. I have respect for the religion—I think the Catholic Church had some excellent liturgists, and I love going to church."

Like many Pagans, he is drawn to ritual and liturgy, which is why he continues to attend church on occasion. What interested Mike in paganism is that it's a very old religion. In fact, he is a Druid because Druidism was an actual religious practice in the ancient world, not something recently invented like Wicca.

Classroom Material

Wicca and witchcraft not only have their own organizations on college campuses today, but they are taught in college classrooms, too. At Georgetown University a class called Witches, History, and Fiction focuses on the history of witchcraft, but at the end of the course, students learn some of the contemporary feminist interpretations of witchcraft. At Brandeis University, the Women's Studies Web site at one time featured a statue of a goddess that would be easily recognized by a practitioner like Carol Christ. At Syracuse University, a course titled Greek Goddesses focuses exclusively on modern feminist Goddess worship and even quotes Carol Christ at the top of the course syllabus. A witchcraft course is also offered in Harvard's Folklore and Mythology Department. The professor told me that he specializes in witchcraft in northern Europe from 1200 to 1500, but in recent years he has had to supplement his academic training with knowledge of neo-Pagan witchcraft not only because of his academic interest in this movement but because of his students' interest in it.

New College of California, a graduate school billed as providing "Education for a Just, Sacred and Sustainable World," offers master's degrees in women's spirituality. Courses are offered on such topics as archaeomythology; women, religion, and social change; and ritual theatre. At the National Women's Studies Association meeting in 2000, neo-Pagan scholar Charlene Spretnak and activist Starhawk were both keynote speakers. Starhawk encouraged women's studies programs to become centers where students can learn the skills they need for being antiglobalization activists.

Despite the presence of these courses and Wiccan and Pagan clubs, many students have to weigh carefully the decision to become Pagan because of discrimination they face on campus.

OSTRACIZED

"Imagine losing all your friends at once," Margaret Ann, a twenty-five-year-old senior who was part of the Pagan club with Cathleen, told me. "I was totally on my own. Soon I went from being angry to just immersing myself in Wicca. I eventually moved to Shamanism, and now I practice Druidism."

Margaret Ann had grown up in the church with very dedicated Baptist parents. She chose to be baptized when she was fourteen. As she got older, however, Margaret Ann realized that one of the main reasons she had joined the church was out of fear of going to hell. She felt that her church never focused on the wonderful aspects of being a Christian, only on the scary effects of not being a Christian. She also loved animals and nature and found that most of her fellow congregants were indifferent when it came to caring for animals and the earth.

"I was born this way, always saving little worms," she told me.

One time in high school, Margaret Ann was at a Christian retreat when a boy in the youth group stoned a snake to death for sport. The other kids just laughed and encouraged him, while Margaret Ann got quite upset. The others could not understand why she cared so much.

Disgusted with her fellow youth-group members' lack of interest in the natural world, Margaret Ann nevertheless joined a well-known national Christian fellowship group when she went to college. She did everything with the group, and all of her friends were part of it. In fact, if you had non-

Christian friends outside of the group, those relationships were called "intentional." Margaret Ann said that on campus the group had a reputation for being cliquish and insular.

One evening at the end of her sophomore year, Margaret Ann saw an ad for the film *Practical Magic* on television. It aroused her curiosity about witchcraft, so she started to look on the Internet for more information. She bought Wiccan books and soon felt as if her heart had arrived home. Wicca emphasized a love of nature, and Margaret Ann felt that it encouraged her love for animals.

"I have always been blunt, so I told others about discovering Wicca. My family ganged up on me and refused to discuss it with me at all."

She left the campus Christian group later that year, and all of her friends, except one, deserted her. Not one of the members of the Christian group bothered to ask why she liked Wicca. No one from the tightly knit worship team she had been a part of would talk to her. She got one anonymous note in her campus mailbox telling her that Jesus loved her. Other Christian students would only talk to her to tell her that they were praying for her. Once Margaret Ann realized her friends were uncomfortable around her, she pulled away from them as well.

Jo was Margaret Ann's one friend who sought her out and asked her about Wicca. "It wasn't only her spiritual community that abandoned her," Jo told me. "People she had known for two years stopped talking to her! I made her go to lunch. Margaret Ann is like a sister to me. When she became a Wiccan, I read up on it, just trying to understand. I realized it was not what I believed, but I concluded that she was not going to kill herself doing it, and I needed to respect her right to believe it."

Despite Jo's friendship and supportive response, Margaret Ann dropped out of school because of the way many of the Christians in the group had treated her, and she returned only after most of her older friends had graduated. Jo left the campus group and began attending a church in town.

I left this interview sickened by the reaction of most of these evangelical Christians when Margaret Ann told them she was interested in Wicca. Both Margaret Ann and Cathleen experienced cruel rejection by the very people who had been taught by Jesus to love and accept others. Cathleen's Catholic parents exhibited no zest or zeal for a relationship with Christ. On the other hand, Margaret Ann's evangelical friends and family showed great religious zeal, but once she began to have doubts about her faith and theirs, they disengaged from any sort of dialogue.

Wheaton College's Mark Noll refers to this unfortunate inconsistency among Christians in his book *The Scandal of the Evangelical Mind,* in which he assesses evangelicalism's strengths and weaknesses. He took another look at evangelicalism in an article for *First Things* in which he concludes that when it comes to Christian learning in America, on one side are those who possess great spiritual energy but often "flounder in putting the mind to use for Christ." On the other side are those who enjoy very rich traditions of learning and Christian thought but often display what he calls a "comatose spirituality."[4]

It's not difficult to see how someone growing up in one of these two cultures might not like either of them and instead choose a third path, such as Wicca. We Christians are intended to live a holistic faith, an integration of evangelicalism and classical Christian doctrine. Noll writes that we are familiar with such terms as "Pentecostal Signs and Wonders" or "Lutheran sacred music." But what if these phrases were common: "Reformed signs and wonders," "intense Lutheran spirituality," "vigorous Catholic evangelism," "Anglo-Catholic devotion to Scripture," and "art history pursued from a Baptist perspective"?[5]

Young people who embrace Wicca are not content with the status quo. For that they have my admiration. They also don't like the boxed categories American Christianity has fallen into. The truth is, the Bible does not define those denominational or evangelical boxes and does not instruct us to force a worldview on someone else. Instead, we must respect other people's worldviews before we can hope to have a dialogue with them. And if, after searching our hearts, we realize that we would rather not engage in constructive dialogue with people who have different worldviews, we need to ask God to change our hearts and minds and fill us with such a desire.

A GREAT MODEL

Cathleen's parents did not take time to understand why she was no longer interested in going to church. Margaret Ann's faith community quoted Scripture at her and reminded her of what Jesus could do for her rather than walking in her shoes for a while.

Fortunately, Jesus provides us with a great model for how to connect with people who have a different worldview from ours: Two blind men approached Jesus seeking healing. Jesus asked them, "Do you believe that I am able to do this?" Their response was, "Yes, Lord." Then he touched their eyes and said, "According to your faith will it be done to you." The Bible says, "Their sight was restored" (Matthew 9:27-30). The startling thing about this story is that Jesus asked the blind men if they believed before he offered healing. Without their faith, he could not heal. Nothing was forced. He respected their worldview.

It's really very simple: Young people are seeking authentic spirituality. We have to respect their model of belief, strange as it may seem to us, before we can expect them to consider ours. As evangelist and author John Stott says in his book *Christian Mission in the Modern World,*

> We cannot sweep away all...cherished convictions with a brash,
> unfeeling dismissal. We have to recognize humbly that some...mis-
> conceptions may be our fault, or at least that [a person's] continuing
> rejection of Christ may be in reality a rejection of the caricature of
> Christ which [the person] has seen in us or in our fellow Christians.[6]

Why should college students seek anything less than authentic spirituality?

—8—

Changing from Within

Wicca in the Church

y church has enjoyed two Wiccan children's directors in the past five years, and Starhawk's prayers and liturgies appear regularly in our order of service," wrote a member of a Methodist church in Austin, Texas, on the church Web site. She calls herself a Methodist witch.

"Confident that I would continue to be welcome in at least one Christian congregation no matter how far afield I ventured [theologically], I opened myself fully to Goddess spirituality for the first time. That fall found me at my first...Samhain, dancing jubilantly by the fire and celebrating my own physicality in a way I never thought I would."[1] To ameliorate the waning number of people in pews in mainline denominations, she recommends that people practice a mixture of Christianity and Paganism at church.

At the Ghost Ranch retreat center in New Mexico, owned by the Presbyterian Church (USA), or PC(USA), women were invited to

> celebrate the sacred feminine Goddess in the Land of Enchantment...With art, movement, ritual and song—Honor the Goddess within each woman. Tell YOUR Herstory with art, voice, dance, ritual. Walk a Hopi labyrinth...Meditate. Create art with your symbolic Goddess language...Dance at the Temple of the Living Goddess. Connect as a sacred circle with very special women for mutual transformation. Share the Magic!!![2]

And some members of the Roman Catholic Church would like to see Paganism practiced during Mass. Two Roman Catholic women in Maryland run an organization called The Women's Alliance for Theology, Ethics and Ritual, or WATER. They publish a quarterly newsletter called *WATERwheel,* and one of its editions quotes Starhawk from the twentieth anniversary edition of *The Spiral Dance.*

Another issue of the newsletter "features a liturgy for All Saints' Day, honoring the gracious Mother Goddess, 'Wisdom—Sophia.'"[3] Participation of a young woman, a middle-aged woman, and an older woman—a crone—is required.

Both women say they hope to transform the church by inducing it to have a more feminist agenda. They say they don't promote Wicca itself but certainly view it as a helpful spirituality for women. WATER is not officially affiliated with the Roman Catholic Church but seeks to influence it and claims to receive funding from a few Catholic bishops.[4]

THE STRUGGLE WITHIN THE CHURCH

My conversations with the people who fill these pages revealed that they all seek a deep, personal, beautiful worship experience and encounter with the Divine. Something about church tugs at their hearts and makes them want to stay in the church even though they don't agree with all Christian teaching.

At first it might seem strange that people would easily mingle neo-Paganism with Christianity. It sounds somewhat preposterous to think of mixing Hinduism, for instance, or the teachings of Islam with Christianity because they clearly contradict each other. But neo-Paganism has no absolutes. Neo-Pagans claim that their spirituality empowers them, affirms the majesty of nature, recognizes the beauty of ritual, and provides a deep, spiritual experience. Unfortunately, they have trouble finding these values in many Christian churches today, so they are trying to change the church from within.

While researching a story several years ago, I encountered a former witch from Salem, Massachusetts. Kathleen had converted to Roman Catholicism many years previously, but because she lived in Salem, she still encountered practicing witches and old friends in the streets. She told me about a Wiccan croning ritual that is practiced in American churches today.

The ritual was documented in a now-defunct journal for Methodist clergywomen in the early 1990s called *Wellspring.* The articles, "A Croning Ritual" and "Reflections from a New Crone," were the eyewitness accounts of two Methodist ministers. Kathleen was surprised the churches were participating in such rituals because a croning ritual is a Wiccan rite of passage.

When the article was published, a group of Methodist clergy became worried about this development. When they contacted one of the authors, she acknowledged having taken part in the ritual and recommended that they read books by Starhawk. The group consulted the bishop of their region, and they reluctantly brought charges against the women according to the Methodist Book of Discipline. During the proceedings, one of the article's authors admitted that the ritual was grounded in Wiccan belief and practice.

Of particular concern was a blessing mentioned at the end of the *Wellspring* article that bore a striking resemblance to a blessing mentioned in Starhawk's *The Spiral Dance,* except that the blessing in *Wellspring* omitted a line about the Goddess. When the bishop asked why this line had been left out, one of the authors said that she had written the blessing from memory and would have inserted the line about the Goddess had she remembered it. In the end no disciplinary action was taken and both women remain at their jobs.

Kathleen told me that she fears that women who practice Goddess worship and Wicca in church don't know what they are doing. "They think they are celebrating their womanhood, but there are darker associations—they should understand what they are dealing with." Kathleen and another ex-witch in Salem named Paula assert that witchcraft is dangerous and real. Paula left Wicca in favor of Catholicism in the 1980s and warns that "magic is real and it works."

Paula told me that she left Wicca because of negative experiences too frightening to describe. She wanted to escape the darkness. But Kathleen and Paula maintain friendships with Wiccans and now share the truth of their own passage with those who will listen.

"These women in the church do not have the discernment we do from the experiences we had," warns Kathleen. "They must be informed."[5]

Women keep attending events such as croning rituals, however, because they are looking for empowerment, a place to redefine God, and a place where they will be accepted. I met with quite a few women who told me that men in the church had never treated them as equally equipped to serve in the church, so they decided to simply invent their own rituals and interpretations of Scripture to mirror more of a feminine perspective. As Kathleen affirmed, most women had no desire to practice anything spiritually dangerous, only to practice their womanhood.

But Donna Hailson, a professor at Eastern Baptist Theological Seminary and recognized authority on neo-Paganism and new spirituality, told me she doesn't think this approach is entirely beneficial for women.

"Many feminists claim that men have interpreted Scripture throughout the centuries in a way that subordinates women and that women should have the chance to change things to better suit their experience," Hailson said. As we saw in chapter 5, Scripture is very affirming of women and gives them equal stature before God. Women don't need to change Scripture; they need to help change the attitudes of those who don't see that or who misuse Scripture for their own gain.

Hailson did point out that much of the feminist literature focuses on the environment, the arts, and new spiritual practices, such as Goddess worship. "This should all serve as a wake-up call to the church to reclaim the arts, to care about the environment, and to show that church is not just a Sunday-morning thing."

SUE MONK KIDD'S FEMININE WOUND

The author of the popular novel *The Secret Life of Bees,* Sue Monk Kidd wrote a lesser-known book titled *Dance of the Dissident Daughter: A Woman's Journey from the Christian Tradition to the Sacred Feminine* in which she describes her journey toward inventing her own rituals and interpreting Scripture to mirror a more feminist perspective.

Kidd had a successful career as an inspirational Christian writer and attended a Southern Baptist church with her family when she began to sense that the role of women in the church was not encouraged as it should be. Once she made a comment to a man at a party about women getting the short end of the stick throughout much of history. The man rolled his eyes and said, "You're not one of *those* women, are you?"

"What women?" she asked.

"One of those screaming feminists always yelling about how bad women have been treated," he replied.[6]

Kidd said that, no, she was not one of those. But as she said it, she felt as if she had trivialized women's experiences. Kidd says that many women carry around a "feminine wound"; they have felt like second-class citizens to men much of their lives and have felt stifled as they have tried to exercise their gifts while acting the part of a good wife or mother. Kidd felt that her wound could be healed by worshiping the Divine Feminine, the Goddess. She found meaning in pagan rituals and conferences.

She tells another story of a conversation with a woman in her church. She suggested that this woman stand up for other women in a church situation, and the woman replied that while that was her desire, she didn't want to look like one of those "fanatical feminists our minister preaches about."

I was saddened when I read of such comments about women being spewed from the pulpit. Aren't God's followers called to listen to those they disagree with, to understand their longings and desires as spiritual seekers? The tragedy is that many Christians scoff at such women—much as I did when I first encountered Wicca. This inattention within the church is part of the reason some professing Christian women and men are turning to Wiccan beliefs and practices.

C. S. Lewis Institute Senior Fellow Art Lindsley likes to say that neo-Paganism has come about as a result of "the unpaid bills of the church." Professing Christian women like Sue Monk Kidd place their spiritual experiences above spiritual truth, despite commandments in Scripture that we should have no other gods but the one true God. Their desperation to feel affirmed as women and their inability to get this need met at some churches propel them to seek affirmation elsewhere.

REIMAGINING GOD

Much of the media attention about Goddess worship in churches first focused on an event called the Re-Imagining Conference, which took place in Minnesota in the early 1990s and was supported at the time by most mainline denominations. Participants at the conference were encouraged to reject traditional notions of Christ's death to atone for sin because "in light of women's experience, such as slavery and female sexual abuse, under-standings of sacrifice, atonement and martyrdom are being re-examined."[7]

According to a report by Methodist clergy who attended, as many as 2,200 conference participants shared in a communion of milk and honey and recited a feminist liturgy: "To our maker Sophia, we are women in your image, with nectar between our thighs we invite a lover, we birth a child, with our warm body fluids we remind the world of its pleasures and sensations."

Sophia was honored at the conference as "our creator Sophia." "Sophia" is the Greek translation of the Old Testament word for wisdom. Some feminist philosophers claim that wisdom is portrayed as a woman in the book of Proverbs and is equal to the God of the Trinity.

Most churches have withdrawn their funding of the continuing Re-Imagining Conferences, but many women from mainline denominations still attend. I believe that the evangelical church needs to engage these women in constructive dialogue. Much of what they believe and practice seems to elevate the experiences of women over Christ, so it makes one wonder how much of what they do is truly "Christian." Removing Christ from Christianity leaves behind an empty religious husk that can be filled with anything.

At the same time, it is vital that the church ask for forgiveness for the many ways it has failed and been unfaithful to these women. Christians should not expect a particularly warm reception, but they will usually be granted a hearing. As John Stott says in his book *Christian Mission in the Modern World,* "If we do nothing but proclaim the gospel to people from a distance, our personal authenticity is bound to be suspect.... But when we sit down alongside them like Philip in the Ethiopian's chariot, or encounter them face to face, a personal relationship is established.... It is recognized that we too are human beings, equally sinful, equally needy, equally dependent on the grace of which we speak."[8]

REPLACING THE HOLY SPIRIT

The Episcopal Church has had its own struggles over neo-Paganism in the church. In particular at the 2000 General Convention, the national church published a booklet called *Resources for Jubilee.* The well-designed booklet was intended to provide thoughtful articles for attendees. The lead article was an innocuous one about Celtic Christianity by Esther de Waal. However, tucked into the center of the booklet was the magazine *Spirituality and Health.* Trinity Church, Wall Street, an Episcopal church in New York City, is the main financier of this magazine, but according to *Spirituality and Health,* the church has no editorial sway over its content. One article in *Spirituality and Health* described Starhawk's Reclaiming witchcamps in detail: "We know about vacation Bible school and Jewish summer camps, but you may not have heard of the growing number of Reclaiming witchcamps." In an article titled "Yes, Dorothy, Witchcamp Is Probably Coming to Kansas," the author explains what they explore at witchcamps:

The pentacle, a five-pointed star used as a meditative balancing tool, is often associated with the head, arms, and legs of the human body or the five stages of life (birth, initiation, maturity, reflection, and death/rebirth). This symbol emphasizes the interconnectedness of many points, rather than a polarized thinking system of good/evil or black/white.[9]

Also in the booklet was an article penned by the director of Trinity Institute, part of Trinity Church, Wall Street. Titled "A Shamanic Journey into the Underworld," the piece chronicles this man's experience with a shaman and his consequent encounter with a raccoon spirit guide that took him back to his childhood when he played with an orphaned raccoon named Oscar. He wrote that the experience into the underworld had metaphorical resonance with the death and resurrection of Jesus.

These articles caused controversy at the General Convention of the Episcopal Church because delegates felt that such spiritual practices and beliefs were incompatible with Anglican Christian doctrine: To deny good and evil would be to misunderstand the entire reason for Jesus's death and resurrection.

In her letter at the beginning of the booklet, the convention director had written,

> I am grateful to the Parish of Trinity Church Wall Street for their collaboration on this resource. Many of the articles in this booklet were originally published in their magazine *Spirituality & Health*, and we include a copy of the most recent issue as another point of connection with this Jubilee event.[10]

The booklets were removed from the convention after complaints from delegates.

I talked over the phone with the author of the raccoon-guide story about his experience. He told me that he did not think his experience was incompatible with the Christian faith, nor did he think it to be animism or Paganism—only guided meditation. He was not one to engage in meditation as a practice and was utterly surprised that this ritual worked.

"There isn't any standard Christian ritual that allows you to go through something like this," he told me. "This ritual was very therapeutic for me." But what about the Holy Spirit, whom Christians have experienced for millennia?

He acknowledged that the Holy Spirit was able to guide and heal people in a similar, powerful way but told me that he had not personally experienced such a thing. He said he felt entirely responsible for what he experienced but did warn that such practices could be frightening if used by people who are unsure of what they are doing.

"I think much of institutionalized religion has not met our deep inner needs. But it needs to happen," he told me.

His comment reminded me of an article titled "The Flaw of the Excluded Middle" by Paul Heibert, referenced in Asbury Theological Seminary professor George Hunter's book *The Celtic Way of Evangelism*. According to Hunter, Heibert argued that human beings have always lived their lives on three levels. The bottom level is empirical. At this level people build a house, fish, or plant crops. The top level is transcendent or sacred. At this level people grapple with the ultimate questions of life, society, and the universe. The middle level, so often excluded by Western churches, especially since the Enlightenment, tends to deal with present crises or the near future. For instance, knowledge about how to plant crops or the real-ization of our small place in the universe is all well and good until a flood washes away the crops and a man's family is left starving. At that point he needs spiritual support. This middle level is inhabited by spells, omens, luck, and traditional folk religions.[11]

Unfortunately, as I mentioned previously, many who attend mainline Christian churches, such as the author of the raccoon spirit-guide article, find that their churches often neglect to deal with these "middle level" issues as if they were too trifling to bother with. When Christianity ignores these issues, we observe "Split-Level Christianity" in which, as Hunter puts it, "people go to church so they can go to heaven, but they also visit, say, the shaman or the astrologer for help with the pressing problems that dom-inate their daily lives."[12]

If traditional Western Christian practices hold no interest for post-modern people, then perhaps the church should think of other ways to reach them. Jesus is the perfect example of this. He met people exactly where they were and often addressed their immediate needs, such as hun-ger or illness, first. Hunter suggests that Celtic Christianity can be a way to reach the Western church again with the truth of Christ's gospel.

CELTIC CHRISTIANITY

As we saw in chapter 2, on Saint Patrick's Day, Matthew Fox and the pro-ducers of the Techno Cosmic Mass used Wiccan and Pagan elements to add a dimension of creativity and spirituality to worship. They celebrated the pagan gods and goddess at the Mass but had no Celtic Christian ele-ments other than a Celtic cross. I think that they—and we—can learn a lot from early Celtic Christians.

The Celtic Christians rid themselves of paganism and were orthodox, yet they maintained a creative dimension to their worship practice. Celtic Christian spirituality was holistic in a way rarely seen in Western churches. Most Western Christians neglect the Celtic Christian practices—indeed, the larger history of Christendom—and confine their church histories to Roman Catholicism and the Reformation. How much they miss!

When Christianity arrived on Ireland's shores in the fifth century, no new religion had existed there for almost one thousand years. The Irish Celts worshiped nature and pagan gods and goddesses, but when Patrick told them about a greater Spirit whom he worshiped, they listened, and many liked what they heard.

Ireland was a largely illiterate society at the time. The Druids, the traditional religious leaders of the Irish Celts, were learned but had closely guarded their knowledge as a way to enhance their status in society. Christianity appealed to the pagan Celts because it was open to all; leaders kept no secrets from the people. As Christ had demonstrated, everyone was welcome.

Anyone who has studied the Celtic pantheon knows it is complex. The Celts were fascinated with rhetorical triads and the number three. The concept of shape shifting—the idea that a deity might appear in various forms—was an accepted concept. Their goddess Brigid is called the triple goddess. Not only is she the goddess of smithcraft (the work of a blacksmith), but she is also the goddess of healing and fire. This worldview made Christianity's triune God seem very accessible and believable. Christianity also engaged the Celtic love of heroism and story, provided affirmation of the Celtic love of nature by celebrating how God's glory is reflected in the world, and confirmed the nearness of the Divine through the Holy Spirit.

Until the arrival of Christianity and its concepts of justice, slavery had been rife in pagan Ireland. Patrick was the first to publicly preach against the evils of slavery, based on the Christian concept that all humans have dignity because we are made in the image of God. As a result of his efforts, slavery was abolished within half a century. Soon much of the violence and intertribal warfare that had characterized the Irish Celts gave way to peace, community, and generosity as the gospel spread across the country.

Because the Celts did not live in established villages and towns as in the Roman Empire and in Europe, they easily took on the Christian concept of community by building monasteries, which were often presided over by abbesses as well as abbots. The Celts believed in the concept of a team. A group of people could encourage one another and keep one another from the loneliness of working individually.

Many of the monasteries were built in beautiful places. Clonmacnoise monastery, built in the eleventh century, overlooks the river Shannon. Although the Vikings sacked Clonmacnoise in the Middle Ages, many of the buildings remain today. Dark gray stone buildings, Celtic crosses, and a worship area sit nestled in a green meadow atop an outcrop that overlooks the river, which stretches into the distance as far as the eye can see.

This would have been a very busy place in its day. Inhabitants would have engaged in long periods of silence for meditation and reflection. For this purpose, they often built cells or huts in remote places away from the community. They were guided by a spiritual director and usually participated in the life of the community through a smaller group if the community was large. The purpose of this lifestyle was to ground and comfort believers and to show God's immanence through the Holy Spirit by living so close to nature. They invited visitors to fellowship with them, converse with them, and be served by them. Many visitors came to faith through these kinds of communities.

A LIGHT IN IRELAND

In a comparatively short time, Ireland went from an illiterate, warring, slave-owning society to a peaceful, community-oriented, literate society. While the rest of Europe was experiencing the Dark Ages and a decline in learning, Ireland was flourishing. Sacred Christian texts and important documents were preserved by these communal monks. A perfect example is the Book of Kells—the four Gospels that were preserved in illuminated manuscripts in the early 800s. The Irish were able to adopt Christianity without denying or abandoning their native culture.

The Celtic Christians' incorporation of their spirituality into their daily lives would appeal to modern seekers who attended Matthew Fox's Techno Cosmic Mass. Unlike their pagan and pantheistic forebears, the Celtic Christians did not worship nature itself or ask for help from nature; rather, they used it as a metaphor to ask for God's help in daily life and in their personal relationships. The Celtic Christians had an oral tradition of prayers and blessings for every part of life—from season to season, daybreak to sundown, and birth to death. Here is part of a Celtic Christian prayer that a woman would pray as she kindled the fire that would provide her family with warmth and light:

I will kindle my fire this morning
In the presence of the holy angels of heaven…

God, kindle Thou in my heart within
A flame of love to my neighbour,
To my foe, to my friend, to my kindred all,
To the brave, to the knave, to the thrall.[13]

In my travels I encountered Pagans who told me that too few of their former church congregations would dare be so imaginative—perhaps they don't know how to be. Many of the imaginative people may already have left the church for the New Age or neo-Paganism already. And many Christian congregations have lost much of their wonder at nature and its beauty that so enthralls the neo-Pagan. They have much to learn from the Celtic Christians and, indeed, from the early church.

Jesus was often chastised for dining with "sinners" and treating women and the outcasts of Jewish society with dignity. He often withdrew to quiet spots in nature to pray and rest. Indeed, Patrick was admonished by the Roman Church for spending too much time fraternizing with the Pagans. And today few Christian congregations welcome Pagans and Wiccans at all.

Celtic Christians understood the importance of welcoming those of other beliefs while maintaining the truth of the gospel. The Christian church today should also welcome dialogue with Pagans, but, like Jesus, we should take care that the gospel message does not get diluted. When modern churches neglect to do this, spiritual seekers may seek to change the church from within and distort the truth of the gospel.

FOR LOVE OF
THE EARTH

The Need for Creation Care

Helicopters droned overhead as I made my way toward the protesters in Washington Square Park. The World Economic Forum that usually meets in Davos, Switzerland, had relocated itself to New York City in early February 2002 in honor of those killed on September 11. Claiming to be the foremost gathering of leaders committed to improving the state of the world, the forum meets annually. Its critics over the years have claimed that it is nothing more than a networking opportunity for the wealthy to come up with new ways to exploit the global poor and the environment. These critics fear that the poor will be marginalized and the environment ravaged as corporations and global leaders lap up the profits of globalization.

That weekend in 2002, while the forum was taking place at the Waldorf-Astoria, thousands of men and women huddled in one corner of the park protesting the elite gathering of government representatives, international organizations, business representatives, and scientists. From helicopters, the police watched them like hawks circling their prey. After the violence at the G8 Summit in Genoa, Italy, six months earlier, the police were taking no chances. Four months after the September 11 attacks, New York needed no more pain, no more tears, and no more trouble.

The protesters in Washington Square Park, however, were not there to be violent. They were there to do magic and perform a ritual. Everyone from communists to anarchists was invited to participate. The organizers, witches who called themselves the Pagan Cluster, hoped that this event would set the tone for the weekend protests and would energize those involved. The Pagan Cluster issued a call for all Pagans and friends to join them in their actions and called on the power of the earth and the Goddess to sustain them.

I arrived at 5 p.m., just as the witches were setting up. Starhawk was to arrive later to help lead the ritual.

As I wandered through the crowd, various groups attending the ritual handed me fliers advocating their causes. A small white flier from the Earth and Animal Liberation Fronts called for "direct action in support of the struggles of humans and non-humans" against the World Economic Forum, the "cocktail party of the world's politicians and corporate elite [who meet] once a year to discuss new ways of raping the environment, exploiting the world's poor and how to expand the industries of abuse to animals."

"We travel the world doing ritual and magic at these protests," a tall man wearing a sash across his chest told me. Many of the neo-Pagans around me were celebrating the coming of spring and the Irish goddess Brigid.

I came to a group huddled in a circle and asked the woman next to me what they were doing. She was bundled up in a hat and scarf and clutched a strip of orange plastic.

"This is called the forge," she told me, pointing to a blacksmith's anvil fashioned out of cardboard and painted black. "This is the goddess Brigid's forge where people cast their vision for the future."

As we spoke, a young woman holding a cardboard hammer raised it over our heads and ceremoniously brought it to bear on the cardboard anvil beneath. Next to the anvil was a large cardboard cauldron of flames represented by the strips of orange and red plastic.

147

"After each person forges their own vision of the future, they bring the sacred flame to the statue of Lady Liberty and offer it as a gift of themselves, their commitment," the woman explained.

She pointed to a statue of a woman made out of wheat. The wheat-sheaf woman held one hand aloft as she stood on a stand made from cardboard and crepe paper. Beneath the statue was a cardboard torch with the word *liberty* written across it. Votive candles adorned the statue's base.

Nearby, the Revolutionary Communist Youth Brigade had set up camp and had begun calling out its own vision for the future: "The U.S. imperialists want to use this jihad they created and unleashed as an excuse to go in and bomb people in Afghanistan and move in on other countries—to go in and massacre more people," said one of their members. "Five thousand children a month are dying in Iraq, and these people who are up at the Waldorf-Astoria are plotting to make even greater advances off of this war. It's important that people around the world see what's happening here—that we're going to stand with them, and we're not going to let the U.S. rulers pretend that this war is happening in our name."

"We need communism," yelled another young woman as she held a banner featuring a silhouetted man raising a gun aloft in front of the red star of communism. I walked over to her and asked what kind of communism she hoped to bring to New York.

"Any kind," she thundered.

"Do you mean the communism of Stalin or Mao Tse-tung?" I asked.

"Yes, that would be great! That is what we need!" she shouted back at me.

Somewhat startled by this I asked, "Do you know much about their policies and what they did to their people?"

She looked at me and blinked. She was quiet for a minute but then resumed her chant for communism to be established in America.

A reporter from the Associated Press sidled up next to me and asked, "Was she really advocating the policies of Stalin?" When I nodded, he exclaimed, "Oh, to be nineteen!" He chuckled as he walked away.

As I continued to wander through the crowd, a woman from the Pagan Cluster handed me a handwritten flier with the title "Cochabamba Declaration" written across the top. She told me that it was written by a group of Bolivians who rose up to reclaim their water supply after it had been privatized. It affirmed that "water belongs to the earth and all species and is sacred to life, therefore, the world's water must be conserved, reclaimed and protected for all future generations and its natural patterns respected.... Water is best protected by local communities and citizens who must be respected as equal partners with governments in the protection and regulation of water. Peoples of the earth are the only vehicle to promote democracy and save water."

Hundreds of people thronged the park. Pagans, anarchists, communists, and the media were crowded onto a raised pavement platform for the ritual. The sense of community among the protesters was palpable; the police and media did not seem to bother them. "By the time we had circled and begun grounding—sinking our roots deep into the Mother and then twining them around each other—we didn't care how many we were or that the people and the press outnumbered us," commented one of the coordinators a week later on their Listserv. "Our work was to do deep magic, to embody our values, to put ourselves on the line."

All of the protesters were invited to take part in the pagan ritual led by Starhawk. The ritual began when someone started a slow beat on a drum. Starhawk began to call out the elements: "Air! Fire!"

The crowd repeated her words.

The witches had set up shrines at different corners of the raised platform.

Participants in the ritual walked from one shrine to the next. In one corner was a shrine for grief. This was the first shrine of the ritual. People could enter, light candles, and remember any deceased loved ones or those who had died on September 11. Other shrines included those for rage, healing, and vision.

Soon the drums became quiet, but the Revolutionary Communist Youth Brigade kept up their chants. A circle gathered around Starhawk. A young woman with her hair in braids stepped into the center of the circle. She wore metal chains around her neck and lighted them so that flames burned at the ends. Then she began to dance as the chains of fire swirled around her.

Soon one of the witches began to chant, and those in the circle chimed in:

> We will never…
> lose our way
> to the well
> of liberty!
> And the power
> of her living flame
> It will rise
> It will rise again!

As the people in the circle chanted, they began to dance. Round and round they went as their chants, led by the witches, rose higher and higher. From my research I knew that the circle was a "spiral dance," traditionally used by witches to raise energy and "a cone of power." The organizers intended it to create energy to sustain the marches and protests for the following day.

After the dance ended, the group—oddly enough, I thought—began to sing a Christian children's song about spreading the gospel: "This little light of mine, I'm gonna let it shine…"

The Pagan Cluster took part in the main demonstrations with other antiglobalization activists during the remainder of the weekend in New York, and after a march on Saturday, a number of Pagans gathered at Grand Central Station. Deciding to do a spiral dance, they joined hands and began to sing their chant from the previous night.

"We will never, never lose our way to the well of liberty, and the power of her living flame, it will rise, it will rise again," they chanted again, referring to the goddess Brigid's flame. Soon riot police attempted to break up the circle. Anarchists joined the dance, and spectators gathered. Like the night before, the participants raised their "cone of power."

As the dance ended, someone began to sing "Amazing Grace"—the hymn that speaks about how Christianity changed the life of former English slave owner John Newton. The choice of this hymn was unusual, given its Christian content, but perhaps the Pagans chose to sing it because it's the closest we in the West have to an indigenous spiritual song. Its sweet, mournful lyrics about going from blindness to sight and from death to life through the power of Christ's resurrection touch people's souls in the deepest places.

I thought of this later as I read Starhawk's reflections on the Friday-night event. She wrote on her Web site that she thought the weekend event had been successful; she hoped that their ritual had woven magic that would bring about transformation.

Transformation. We all want the blind to see, the wretched to be saved.

Wiccans and neo-Pagans are looking for change in a crazy world, and they see political protest as a natural outgrowth of their spiritual hunger and beliefs. As "Amazing Grace" suggests, we each have a desire to shine "as the sun" and live peacefully in community with others. Since Wicca seems to suit both spiritual needs and political predilections, it has provided a sense of purpose for some who are weary not just of church but of government decisions that seem to compromise the world they long for.

WHAT MOTIVATES THEM?

The confluence of activists and Pagans is no coincidence. Across the country hundreds of covens are forming affinity groups of their own. As young people jettison traditional faiths, they seek something to fill their spiritual void that also offers tangible goals. Wicca or Paganism engages them spiritually and often meets their political preferences as well.

The Pagan Cluster present at the 2002 WEF protests also calls itself the Living River. Its goal is to bring attention to issues of water and to embody the element of water under fire. The Pagan Cluster/Living River is made up of a core of Pagans who travel all over the world demonstrating at conferences such as the World Economic Forum, the International Monetary Fund (IMF) meetings, G8 Summits, the World Trade Organization (WTO), and World Bank meetings. To protest the Free Trade Area of the Americas (FTAA) meeting in Quebec City in April 2001, for example, Starhawk and others in the Pagan community sensed the need for action of their own. They chose the name "Living River" for the Quebec protests to draw attention to the water issues being discussed at the FTAA. The name remains.

Wherever they go, the Pagan Cluster/Living River casts spells, makes magic, and performs rituals like the one in Washington Square Park. Many other antiglobalization activists, such as the anarchists and communists, join them in these endeavors. The Pagan Cluster/Living River is motivated by the views of neo-Pagan witchcraft: that the earth is sacred, and the great Mother Goddess manifests herself in the forms of many goddesses, such as Brigid. Many members have roots in the Reclaiming tradition of witchcraft and identify with Reclaiming principles: "Understanding that the earth is alive and all of life is sacred and interconnected. We see the Goddess as immanent in the earth's cycles of birth, growth, death, decay and regeneration. Our practice arises from a deep, spiritual commitment to the earth, to healing and to the linking of magic with political action."[1]

The Pagan Cluster/Living River also joined in the Pagan protest against a G8 Summit in Canada. A small group of Reclaiming witches gathered to work their magic. Just weeks before the event, this e-mail appeared on the Living River Listserv:

> We need your help. There are three basic ways we are asking for
> magic support. Trancework: On Saturday night, June 22, between
> the solstice and the full moon we will be doing a group trance.
> We are only a few Reclaiming Witches physically present here. But
> together with our extended community, we can be a powerful force
> in the magical world. When we link up, we make a difference.

They asked others to "support us with magical shielding, or meet us on the astral and help us enter the fortress, identify its vulnerabilities, uproot its anchor, disrupt its magic."

After the protest, one member of the Pagan Cluster who participated in the ritual wrote on the Listserv,

We are engaged in a battle right now, an immense struggle that will determine the future of our world. Whatever happens on the streets, whatever weapons and armies are massed, ultimately it is a battle of hearts and minds and consciousness, a struggle between fear and love. This is the territory we know and the ground we can stand on in our power as Witches.

To join the Pagan Cluster/Living River, one does not have to be Pagan but must realize that the Cluster does engage in pagan rituals and spiritual practices, including divination. The group claims to be nonauthoritarian and nonhierarchical. It also claims to build bridges and open channels of communication between many diverse groups.

As we've seen, Starhawk is a prominent leader among antiglobalization activists. She joined the antiglobalization protests first in 1999 in protest of the WTO meetings in Seattle, and she has been part of the movement ever since. Now her spiritual beliefs seem to be affecting a much larger group of people.

In her books Starhawk makes it clear that her witchcraft influences her political actions. In *Dreaming the Dark,* she defines magic as "the art of evoking power-from-within and using it to transform ourselves, our community, our culture, using it to resist the destruction that those who wield power-over are bringing upon the world."[2] She draws on the popular radical feminist historical interpretation of the witch trials, or burning times, as an example when power was wielded over the peasants and their connection to the land. The need to reclaim the land and the livelihood of these peasants and peoples of the world is what propels Starhawk in her witchcraft and political actions. She believes that by using magic, we change not just ourselves but the world as well. She promotes relaxed sexual standards; indeed, she encourages all sorts of experimentation as a way to tap into the greater magical energy of the universe. She envisions witches as changing the planet for the better.

"The ritual, the magic, spins the bonds that can sustain us to continue the work over years, over lifetimes," she writes. "Transforming culture is a long-term project. We organize now to buy time, to postpone destruction just a little bit longer in the hope that before it comes, we will have grown somehow wiser—somehow stronger—so that in the end we will avert the holocaust.... If we cannot live to see the completion of that revolution, we can plant its seeds in our circles, we can dream its shape in our visions, and our rituals can feed its growing power." Starhawk is a classic pantheist—all is the Divine; all is One.

"As we see the Goddess mirrored in each other's eyes, we take that power in our hands as we take hands, as we touch. For the strength of that power is in the bond we make with each other. And our vision grows strong when we no longer dream alone."[3]

The Belief Behind the Protest: Gaia Spirituality

Under the growing influence of Starhawk and the Reclaiming movement, neo-Pagan witchcraft activism has an underpinning worldview: Gaia spirituality. Gaia was the earth goddess for the ancient Greeks, but with the rise of neo-Paganism, she has become a central figure in the new spirituality of the earth.

Renowned British scientist and environmentalist James Lovelock is most responsible for introducing Gaia into our modern lexicon. In the early 1970s he proposed the theory that the earth was a living being—that everything on earth from whales to rocks was part of one organism. Gaia, the earth, self-regulates so that the sea retains the correct level of salinity to sustain life, the atmosphere has the perfect amount of oxygen, and so on. After several years of living and working in the States, Lovelock returned to England where he erected a stone statue of Gaia in his garden. Lovelock's theory created a following of people who believe that we must embrace Goddess worship in order to appease Gaia and maintain earth's delicate balance of life.

This is where the Gaia hypothesis links up to Wicca and Goddess worship. This is also the nexus for political activist witches like Starhawk. Whether or not she or other witches fully embrace the Gaia hypothesis, they have certainly been influenced by it.

Like political feminism, ecological activism offered political gains to activists but held little in the way of spiritual sustenance. Lovelock's view of the earth as a sacred goddess offers a more spiritual component to feminist protests. Many diverse antiglobalization groups such as anarchists and antireligious communists take part in Starhawk's rituals because the participants honor the Goddess. The popularity of Wicca and Goddess worship coincides nicely to create a new worldview. The rituals provide spiritual sustenance when the ideologies they support, particularly communism, have none. To communists, environmental activists, and antiauthoritarian activists, the church or any organized religion is the enemy. Neo-Pagan spirituality is an alternative that embraces their beliefs about both politics and the environment.

In her book *Webs of Power,* Starhawk echoes the Gaia theory:

> There is another view...held by most indigenous cultures, by
> bioreligionists and permaculturalists and many people who live
> closer to the earth—and that is to see humans as being ourselves

as much nature as any old-growth redwood, mosquito, or wild-flower. We are, in fact, animals. We are bodies evolved over billions of years to eat…breathe, drink, reproduce, die, and decay like other bodies. In nature, every giant whale and tiny microorganism has a role to play in the balance of the whole. How arrogant to think that we don't![4]

Because neo-Pagans believe that humans are not separate from nature—we are an integrated part of it, no more special than a rock, tree, whale, or ostrich—we are compelled to play a role in maintaining the balance of life. A question pantheists often ignore, however, is this: How can we compel people to care for the earth and nature if there is no higher moral authority to which humans must answer? If humans are no different from a rock or tree, what is to stop a logging company from not only logging the trees but mowing down protesters who might try to block them? Most Wiccans and Pagans with whom I spoke seemed unconcerned by this question; they failed to take into account the darker side of human nature. Paganism worked for them as a form of protest against the ills of the world, and it did not matter whether their spirituality functioned on a broader philosophical level.

One of my recurring questions for witches was "What would you do if you were president and had to make difficult decisions? How would your spirituality affect this?" Just like Marisa in Salem, they had a consistent response governed by situational ethics. A surprising number responded by saying, "I would just channel energy toward the problem" or "I'm not president—it's not my problem."

The majority of Pagans in North America are well educated, white, and upper middle class. They are a new movement. Unlike the Native Americans, they have no instant affiliation with an indigenous Pagan group. Desperate to have an earth religion of their own, they have created their own pagan identity. They are a group that longs for justice and community in this world, and becoming Pagan is one way they try to bring about change.

The startling thing is that, in the end, what Pagans call for socially and politically is not that different from what Jesus taught. Although it may surprise members of the Pagan Cluster, politically their ideas are conservative in the traditional sense of the word—the importance of democracy, citizen empowerment, local control of resources, and the right to life. The difference is, of course, that for neo-Pagan protesters, the earth is their divine entity. It is their god—or goddess. Casting spells and participating in rite and ritual are the only spiritual ways they know to try to save it.

NO MORE SENSE OF PLACE

The prominence that Wiccans and neo-Pagans give antiglobalization suggests that many Westerners want to make a spiritual practice of trying to recover our sense of place, our rootedness. In her book *Webs of Power,* Starhawk writes,

> Indigenous cultures around the world, including those we draw
> from in our present-day Pagan traditions, have seen themselves as
> part of nature.…
>
> All of our ancestors were indigenous to somewhere; that is, they
> were deeply rooted in one place, living in a culture in which suste-
> nance, spirit, and culture arose from the plants, animals, climate,
> and resources of that particular land. If we are going to create a new
> political/economic/social system, one that truly cares for the environ-

ment and for human beings, we may need to become indigenous again, to find at least one spot on the earth we can know intimately.[5]

In today's transient culture, often we don't know our neighbors or much about our communities. We have no idea how we get our water or what type of soil is under the grass of the front lawn. It is easy to exploit the land when you don't know anything about it. This is what Starhawk and other neo-Pagans have noticed, and their activism is an attempt to do something about it.

The philosopher Martin Heidegger wrote that place positions "man in such a way that it reveals the external bounds of his existence and at the same time the depths of his freedom and reality."[6] To lose this aspect of life can cause us to feel adrift in the world—without mooring or grounding.

In her book *The Need for Roots,* French writer Simone Weil stated,

To be rooted is perhaps the most important and least recognized need of the human soul. It is one of the hardest to define. A human being has roots by virtue of his real, active and natural participation in the life of a community which preserves in living shape certain particular...expectations for the future.... Every human being needs to have multiple roots. It is necessary for him to draw wellnigh the whole of his moral, intellectual and spiritual life by way of the environment of which he forms a natural part.[7]

Weil writes that having roots in a place meets the "needs of the soul."

Environmentalist and author Alan Durning writes about this sense of rootlessness in his book *This Place on Earth.* As a young researcher for the Washington DC–based Worldwatch Institute, Durning traversed the world.

"I...began hopscotching the globe myself, studying everything from poverty to atmospheric chemistry," he writes. "It was urgent stuff: documenting injustice, testifying before Congress, jet-setting on behalf of future generations."

On one of these trips Durning was in the Philippines interviewing members of a remote hill tribe. A tribal elder had showed Durning the land that they had tended for centuries. The elder then introduced Durning to an old woman who was revered as a traditional priestess.

"What is your homeland like?" she asked through an interpreter.

Durning did not know what to say. "Should I tell her about my neighborhood on the edge of Washington, D.C., the one where I then lived with my wife, Amy, and our son, Gary? The one where we could not let Gary play outside our apartment because of the traffic?"

"Tell me about your place," the woman repeated.

Durning writes of his realization that he lacked any connection to his base in Washington DC. "And for some reason...it shamed me. I had breakfasted with senators and shaken hands with presidents, but I was tongue-tied before this barefoot old woman."

He answered her question, "'In America we have careers, not places.'

"Looking up, I recognized pity in her eyes."[8]

Durning ended up leaving his life as a world traveler and returned to the Pacific Northwest, where he had lived as a child. He settled there with his family, determined to sink roots into the area and find his sense of place.

Edward Relph, author of the book *Place and Placelessness,* declares that there has been a separation of humankind from landscape and nature. Industrialized humans have the ability to build everywhere, so connections to the land are lost. Mile after mile of concrete and subdivisions create a soulless community. Our current loss of connection to land is the first of its kind to take place in history on such a grand scale. It had no precedent prior to the 1800s. Coincidentally, the rise of the industrialized West in the mid-nineteenth century is when Swiss-German historian J. J. Bachofen first proposed the idea of the matriarchy and when the ideas that form the basis of Wicca were kindled.

Interestingly, Christianity is growing rapidly in Third World countries that have been traditionally pagan. There, out of necessity, the population is more connected to the land, but they have realized that the land and nature around them will not save them even though their pagan religions have tried for millennia to appease nature.

Meanwhile, the West is embracing the Paganism that many in the Third World are leaving behind. Religious scholar Phillip Jenkins reported in the *Atlantic Monthly* that "by 2025, 50 percent of the Christian population will be in Africa and Latin America, and another 17 percent will be in Asia. Those proportions will grow steadily."[9]

In the United States, we are wealthy and disconnected from the land, so we can romanticize that it is better and purer than we are. But we are much more sheltered from its fierce consequences. Those who live at its mercy and have lost loved ones to nature's capriciousness need a God who says, "This is not how it was meant to be. Fear not, I have overcome death by my death and resurrection. Come to me, all you who are heavy laden, all you who suffer. I am the only Divinity who has been a cosufferer with you. I know and have felt your pain."

There is hope in that message! Unfortunately, neo-Pagans miss Christianity's true essence and protest the Christian faith as an extension of Western corporate globalization and imperialism.

What's a Christian to Do?

Starhawk's words are powerful and sometimes sound militant. But what she really wants is justice, something that Wicca on its own can never bring about. In fact, many of the longings of Pagan activists—for hope, redemption, stewardship of the earth's resources, justice, and community—are not that different from the longings of Christians. It should not be hard for Christians to identify with Pagans and respond to their concerns. But surprisingly few Christians in the United States take these issues seriously. Most of us are into personal piety—going to church, reading the Bible, and praying. Sure, we donate our time and money to various social causes, but do most of us think about the fact that well-known clothing chains use slave labor to manufacture their products? Sure, those people have jobs they might not have had otherwise, but is everything good about that? As followers of Jesus, we have a responsibility to think seriously about these issues.

One group of people I know carefully consider these issues from a Christian perspective. The group is called A Rocha, which means "the rock" in Portuguese. A British vicar named Peter Harris began the group in the early 1980s with a field-studies center and a bird sanctuary on Portugal's Algarve Coast. Harris and his family were committed to recovering a biblical approach to the study and care of creation. Since then, A Rocha's work has expanded to several other countries, including Lebanon, Kenya, England, the United States, and Canada. Evangelist John Stott, among others, has been a longtime supporter of A Rocha.

A Rocha defines itself in five ways (the "5 Cs"): Christian, conservation, community, cross-cultural, and cooperation. Members are motivated by their biblical faith and by God as Creator to focus on conservation of

God's planet through the scientific study of plant and animal life. The Alvor Estuary in Portugal is home to millions of birds, endangered species, and a large variety of plant and insect life, including a moth previously unknown to science. A Rocha seeks to work with the local community to balance its needs with sound conservation. All scientists, students, and conservationists who live and work at the project live in community with one another, sharing much of what they have.

In London, A Rocha is situated in the heavily urbanized area of Southall. Much of the local population is from South Asia—Sikhs, Hindus, and Muslims. Parts of Southall suffer from some of the worst overcrowding and lack of green space in Europe. A Rocha's project is called Living Waterways. It has committed to study and protect a ninety-acre area of publicly owned land and turn it into a community resource—a country park with a field-study center. The group has had strong community involvement at all levels and has also introduced environmental education in local schools.[10]

I met Peter Harris in Washington while he was visiting the United States. His passion for his work was evident. Unlike some environmentalists, he was not strident or shrill in his language. He gently spoke about our need to care for what God created.

"It is very biblical to care for the creation. As Cal DeWitt has pointed out, we may love God, but we can't say we love Rembrandt and trash his paintings," he said with a smile. He told me that A Rocha occasionally has neo-Pagans living within its various centers.

"We recently had a family of neo-Pagans living at our Portuguese community," he told me. "We welcome them, but we are very explicit about our Christian beliefs. While we don't agree with their worldview, we know that they can make a valuable contribution to our projects. Many of these people are highly talented and principled in many ways." The neo-Pagans who live at A Rocha respect the organization's Christian beliefs and are willing to abide by certain community standards during their time there.

Peter spoke passionately about the apostle Paul preaching to the pagans in Athens and taking time to learn about their poets. Paul used their shared interests to describe God, Jesus, and what Jesus's death and resurrection really means.

"This is what we try to do at A Rocha. There is no dividing wall between Christians and Pagans—no 'us versus them,'" he insisted. "Too often we build walls between us. While we do have different beliefs, there is no reason why Pagans and Christians can't love one another. Christians are commanded to love Pagans, but they often do a poor job of it."

A Rocha's broader commitment is to provoke Christians to read the Bible and examine their theology. Dave Bookless, an evangelical Anglican minister who runs A Rocha UK, points out that A Rocha's work challenges the "philosophical dualism that has so dogged Western Christendom, and has led many Christians to care only for 'saving souls.'… The Biblical drama tells of a God who delights in the act of creation, makes humanity from dust, and has a covenant with the earth itself (Genesis 9); a God who takes material flesh upon himself, undergoes a bodily resurrection, and promises a renewed heavens and earth."[11]

Bookless discovered while studying New Testament Greek that the word for "world" in John 3:16 ("For God so loved the world that he gave his one and only Son, that whoever believes in him shall not perish but have eternal life") is actually the Greek word *kosmos,* the same word we use today—*cosmos.* God so loved the whole universe, the cosmos, that he sent his only Son. Some scholars argue that kosmos could mean "world of men," but the apostle Paul echoed that Jesus's earthly mission resulted in major consequences for the earth itself. Bookless writes,

In Colossians 1:15-21, [Paul] describes Jesus as creator of all and saviour of all—not just people, but that "God made peace through his Son's sacrificial death on the cross and so brought back to himself all things both on earth and in heaven" (v.21). All things! In Romans 8.19-23, Paul talks of the whole creation groaning with pain, like a woman about to give birth—but also groaning in hope—the hope "that creation itself would one day be set free from its slavery to decay and would share the glorious freedom of the children of God" (v.21). In these passages we have clearly what John 3.16 only hints at: God made it. God loves it, and in Jesus God is saving his creation.[12]

It doesn't take much to begin to care for creation and be a good steward of God's resources. Simple projects like writing creative Sunday-school curricula or working to restore a local wilderness area would go a long way toward helping children understand the importance of creation care. Another idea is to take young people on a camping trip where they can learn to identify local flora and fauna as they study what Scripture says about creation.

A Rocha lives simply in sustainable community, as Jesus did. Jesus cared deeply for the poor and the downtrodden and expected no less from his followers. A Rocha understands this, Celtic Christians understood this, the early church understood this—indeed, this is Christianity. But when modern churches neglect these core values, many spiritual seekers turn to a pagan belief system that appears to stand up for the environment, the underprivileged, and the marginalized. Wiccans are looking for an authentic, embodied spirituality, and this is what Jesus called his followers to as well.

QUENCHING THE
SOUL THIRST

One crisp autumn morning five years after that first magazine assignment led me to report on Wicca, I went to our local bookshop to buy a gift. As I glided up the escalator to the second floor, my gaze fell upon the shelves of calendars for the new year. I noticed how many of them had Wiccan or neo-Pagan themes. Five years earlier I would have been appalled that such things were being sold in my local bookshop. I would have seen them as a sign that our culture is in a continual downward spiral away from God. When I noticed them that morning, though, I was not alarmed.

Shortly thereafter I smiled when I learned that the daughters of a friend of mine had a Wiccan classmate. At least she had a desire to worship something. She was looking for answers in life that went beyond our secular culture. This was good. This was the place to start in dialogue with her about faith and spirituality. This young woman was displaying what C. S. Lewis called *"sehnsucht,"* meaning a longing for the mysterious and the wonderful.[1] "Our lifelong nostalgia," he wrote, "our longing to be reunited with something in the universe from which we now feel cut off, to be on the inside of some door which we have always seen from the outside, is no mere neurotic fancy, but the truest index of our real situation."[2]

So I didn't take either of these circumstances as a sign that people are interested in stranger and more bizarre things these days. What I did see is that people are realizing that there is more to this life than the mechanized culture in which we live, and they want answers to quench the thirst in their souls, their "sehnsucht." French mathematician and philosopher Blaise Pascal calls this thirst our longing to fill the "God-shaped void" in our lives. In other words, we are made to want something more than this life.

Scripture says that the deepest longing of the human heart is to know and enjoy the glory of God. Indeed, we were created for this reason: that God might "make the riches of his glory known to the objects of his mercy" (Romans 9:23). In the same way a baby is made for dependence on her parents or parents long to teach their children about all the good and glorious things in life, God, too, has created his children to know his glorious riches, of which, as John Piper puts it, "the untracked, unimaginable stretches of the created universe are a parable about the inexhaustible 'riches of his glory.' "[3]

Neo-Pagan men and women, Wiccans, witches, and Goddess worshipers are a step ahead of many in our secular culture in acknowledging their longings and trying to fulfill them. As I researched this book, these seekers had a profound impact on me, although I consistently disagreed with them. They were edgy and earthy, thoughtful and artistic, flamboyant and wild and wounded. Their eyes beheld the created universe as a lovely metaphor for *something else*. They have decided it is the spirit world—gods and goddesses who are metaphors for the great Goddess who is embodied in us. Unlike Christians, neo-Pagans don't see God. They miss the mark. The word *sin,* in fact, means just that: "missing the mark." Neo-Pagans aren't the only ones to miss the mark. Christians also often miss the mark by condemning neo-Pagans without knowing anything about them and not recognizing that many are actually on a path that might lead them to God.

Because of my interaction with neo-Pagans, my eyes have been opened even more to the beauty of nature, and I am more concerned about caring for creation than I was when I began this book. I also know that the churches that dismiss, ignore, or don't have time for the Holy Spirit lose members to alternative spiritualities that embrace the supernatural. I know that a church that strips Jesus of his divinity and simply calls him a "good man" risks sentencing its members to lives of desperate frustration as they rely on themselves and not on the power of Jesus for betterment. I know that churches whose members recite formulaic phrases in an effort to woo people to Jesus won't attract many seekers today. I know that churches that have abandoned Christ's attitude toward women risk damaging women's lives. I know that when churches fail to get to know non-Christians and instead judge them based on the books they read and what they have experienced, these churches risk turning people away from God.

But I also have a much bigger picture of who God is than I did five years ago. This may sound strange, but Wiccans have made my personal faith stronger, because while I have come to understand and empathize with their struggles and religious yearnings, I do not think they have arrived at the answer. Since I was a little girl, I have based my life on the word, life, death, and resurrection of Jesus of Nazareth, and I haven't been swayed in my conviction that what he came to share with us is real and true. I am drawn to him all the more.

The reasons Wiccans have chosen their spiritual paths were similar for every Wiccan I talked to. They long for a sense of community. Women want to feel safe and affirmed in their womanhood. They want somewhere to belong and be loved, not condemned. They want their spirituality to have more of a focus on caring for nature. They are seeking a spirituality that is real and has a supernatural element to it. They want a spirituality without absolutes or orthodoxy—one they can make their own. And, finally, many have been wounded in life or by the church and want to escape the place where those wounds were inflicted.

ALISON'S STORY

These certainly were the reasons that Alison was drawn to Wicca as a college sophomore. My conversations with Alison were some of the most powerful and intriguing I had in the course of my research.

Born in Berkeley, California, in 1960, Alison and her family attended a liberal, social-gospel church throughout her childhood. While her parents and the congregation spent themselves in doing good deeds, Alison longed for the supernatural and more ritual in her religious experience. She was very drawn to Jesus and, like Margot Adler, found herself fascinated with the mystical side of Christianity. She began sneaking off to Catholic Mass when she was ten. She loved the pomp, the smells, and the bells of it all. By her teenage years, however, her spiritual side went underground, and she found meaning in novels and literature instead. She was thrilled to be accepted to Princeton University where her literary interests were further nourished.

Her parents divorced that year, however, and Alison spiraled into a deep depression. She fell into an abusive relationship with a man and became anorexic. She began to feel that if she herself could just disappear, the problems would also go away.

Since Alison's father had abandoned the family and her boyfriend had abused her, Alison soon thought that perhaps women were safer and would not hurt her. At the beginning of her second year at Princeton, her best friend came out as a lesbian, and Alison went with her to the women's center, where lesbians were welcome, to see if she could find a safe community there.

It was there that she was introduced to Goddess worship and Wicca. She participated in Wiccan ceremonies and began to read many books on the topic. Women at the center were syncretists, trying to combine the religion of their upbringing with Wicca. The first Wiccan ceremony Alison attended was led by a Jewish rabbinical student. She found this approach somewhat incoherent and consequently was drawn to the work of Mary Daly, who had turned her back entirely on the Judeo-Christian world. Alison believed that Daly was qualified to do this because of her intellect and multiple doctorates in Catholic theology. In her anger, Alison liked Daly's idea of blaming men for the ills of world. At that time men were the enemy in Alison's life, and Daly saw women as saviors. Alison drew closer to Wicca and the Goddess for their promise of female empowerment. She was looking for a coherent worldview and for acceptance as a woman.

She also liked Wicca because it was similar to her liberal social-gospel church upbringing. It didn't ask much of her. She could perform rituals to satisfy herself, do some good deeds from time to time, and try to better herself. What Wicca had that her church experience had lacked, however, was the supernatural element that had so appealed to her as a child.

Events in Alison's life soon became dissonant. Despite Mary Daly's view of women, Alison quickly learned that women and feminists could be just as manipulative as men. The Christians she met at Princeton also began to frustrate her. Most smirked when she talked about her spirituality. The worst was when they would come over to the Wiccan/feminist table at dinner, sit next to her, and ask, without any inquiry about her personal life, whether she had considered the claims of Jesus Christ. This programmatic approach didn't reach her at all.

Soon no one was relating to her personal struggles. Her Wiccan friends let her down, and her lesbian friends preached against men while continuing to have boyfriends on the football team. While they talked about living a natural lesbian lifestyle, they polluted their bodies by taking drugs on the side. In the midst of this, Alison struggled to build her own pagan religion and continued to read Mary Daly. Even Daly disappointed her at times, though, because despite her encounters with Christians on campus, Alison still had a positive view of Jesus. When in the course of her reading she got to the part where Daly called God a sadist, Alison simply could not agree and found herself starting to pull away from neo-Paganism.

That summer she worked in an office with what she called three "down-to-earth Christian women from the Midwest." On her last day she went to lunch with one of them and tried to bait her about her faith, asking her how she could be a Christian since all Christians hated women and gays. The woman listened to her for a while and when Alison was finished, the woman looked at her and said simply, "You know, the only thing that matters is that you know Jesus is Christ and Lord."

There he was again. Jesus.

After that summer Alison went to study in Spain for a year. She was placed in a family of Catalan Baptists in Barcelona. The first night she was there, Alison poured out her problems to the family and presented her Wiccan views as answers. The mother of the family told her that the answer for her was Jesus.

There he was again. Jesus.

This woman knew what it was like to suffer and feel outcast and alone. She had grown up oppressed, a Protestant in Franco's Spain where all religious expression other than Catholicism was outlawed. She had clung to Jesus during this time. Alison was drawn to this woman's authenticity, so she began to accompany her to church. The minister there was a graduate of Oxford University and was able to answer Alison's questions about faith.

This young Spanish mother also made herself available to Alison as Alison thought through what she believed and why. Within a month of arriving in Spain, Alison decided that she wanted to follow Jesus and the Christian faith. She has not looked back since.

So what did the gospel offer Alison that Wicca never did?

"A future and a hope," she told me without hesitation. "Wicca was always looking back to the matriarchal past. Wicca was all about self-transformation. I needed forgiveness of guilt. The Goddess is remote. The Goddess is not personal. Worshiping her power in the universe was so impersonal. I needed some One. I was impressed that Jesus was so loving and personal."

Alison also realized that neither men nor women would, by themselves, save the world. She had seen her father devote his whole life to doing good works in their social-gospel church without any kind of personal faith. He finally burned out, left his family, and went to find himself. The neo-Pagan women who had provided her with community and love at the women's center ultimately let her down too. And she certainly knew she was tired of her own efforts. Jesus was appealing because he was both earthily human and supernaturally divine. He met her need for a supernatural experience, yet he was a personal God, not some remote deity who didn't care about the universe.

Alison's desire reflects the desire within each of us for the supernatural. In his series of lectures on the holiness of God, theologian R. C. Sproul notes that most of us as children go through a phase when we are fascinated by ghost stories. We can't get enough of them around the scout campfire, at slumber parties, or on the playground. We ask our friends to tell them to us again and again.

I remember as a child huddling with other children inside a big plastic tunnel at day camp and insisting that our counselor tell and retell a story called "The Green Hand." I can't remember what it was about now, only that it sent us squealing out on the playground, chills running up and down our spines, every time we heard it.

Why do we love to hear stories of the supernatural? Sproul says it reflects a longing to see the holiness of God. Augustine, too, spoke of the restlessness in our hearts that will only be satisfied by God in his glory. But we look to so many other things, don't we?

Those who embrace neo-Paganism have found a way to satisfy their desire for holiness. Although they have embraced the occult, their yearning for something more is no different from the spiritual longings of many Christians. I often think of this during Holy Week at our church. The week between Palm Sunday and Easter is a time of great sadness followed by great joy as the Anglican Church, through its liturgy, relives the last week of Christ's life from his triumphal procession into Jerusalem on Palm Sunday to his death on the cross on Good Friday to his resurrection on Easter Sunday. Christians from Bible churches and other less liturgical denominations flock to our Anglican services during this week. They love the ritual that helps them understand again the great sacrifice Christ made. Most of us long for a ritual spiritual experience, whether or not we are aware of it.

WHAT CHRISTIANITY OFFERS

As surprising as this may sound to the Wiccans I've met, I believe that Christianity offers all of what neo-Pagans seek. Neo-Paganism draws more on Christianity than most people realize. Jesus himself embodies much of what neo-Pagans long for: He affirms women; he is real, yet supernatural; and he wants to heal our wounds. Pointing this out might lead to an interesting discussion with a Wiccan friend or neighbor. So now that you know what Wicca is and what draws people to it, I'd like to share some thoughts on what Christianity offers that Wiccans are looking for.

Acquainted with Grief

Peggy Orenstein said that Christianity was seriously lacking when it came to helping her grieve her miscarriage. She is right—there are no specific rituals for a miscarriage, but that doesn't mean that God doesn't care about the pain. God, through his Son, Jesus, is a cosufferer with us in life's deepest sorrows. The gospel message offers hope through the life, death, and resurrection of Jesus.

While writing this book, I, too, suffered a miscarriage. This was our first child, and the loss was the most painful experience I have been through in my life. It is something I will never fully get over; for the days surrounding the miscarriage, I was inconsolable. Like Orenstein, I walked around in a gray haze.

I miscarried at the end of October, just prior to Halloween. In the Anglican tradition, this day is celebrated as All Saints' Day or All Hallows Eve, and our church holds a service each year at this time to remember those who have departed this life. But that year the pastoral clergy had come to realize that many women had experienced miscarriages and stillbirths, but there was no way to acknowledge those lives in the life of the church. When a baby dies, there is a funeral, but when a child dies several months before birth, there is no way to mark or acknowledge that life—a life that is physically very real to the woman from the first day she learns she is pregnant. Therefore, our church dedicated the All Saints' Day service to mourning and memorializing miscarried babies. This occurred not five days after our loss.

I felt drenched in sadness as I entered the sanctuary. Another woman who had suffered two miscarriages handed me a program and a little white angel ornament for our Christmas tree to help us commemorate our baby. The timing could not have been better. The ritual of the service allowed my husband and me to feel some closure and experience a public acknowledgment that our baby was real and that we loved him for the three months he was in my womb. After many tears, we left a little less sad, and we were filled with hope that we would see our baby one day in heaven. This sort of public, communal ritual is what Peggy Orenstein said she longed for.

The neo-Pagan attraction to ritual was all the more understandable in light of our miscarriage. But through this experience I learned spiritual lessons about my own faith that went far deeper than my appreciation for ritual itself.

Because we live in a fallen world, we all experience suffering. As Christians we believe that is not the way it was supposed to be. A parent knows all too well the desire to switch places with a child to spare that child pain. The same sentiment usually exists between loved ones. In the days surrounding my miscarriage, my husband told me over and over again how he wished he were physically going through it, not me. He wished to shoulder my burden. When he went through a difficult surgery, I, too, wished I could spare him the agony.

We are God's children. As our parent God sees and understands our pain. He so much longs to spare us ultimate pain and suffering that he sent his Son to die for us, to redeem us, to lift us out of the miry pit of eternal sin and pain. We will still have suffering in this life, but there is hope because God has overcome sin, sadness, and life's pain. He is acquainted with grief.

In losing our child, I felt as if I got a glimpse of the grief God felt when he sent his only Son to die for us. We know how much we want to spare our loved ones pain, but to have such love for them that we would send our own child to die in their place is almost beyond comprehension. Yet that is what God did through his Trinitarian relationship with Christ.

As human beings we can never understand someone else's pain until we have gone through the same experience ourselves. This is the maddening truth of our human existence. But because Jesus died on the cross, God already understands what we go through—*and then some.*

So instead of asking a god or goddess to appease my particular pain, I found comfort in knowing that God took on the entire pain of humanity when Jesus died on the cross. No goddess, not even the Mother Goddess herself, took on human flesh and suffered human pain as we do. Jesus offers extraordinary hope in a way Wicca can't.

Creation Waits

Neo-Pagans believe that the universe and nature represent something greater than themselves, something worth worshiping. The belief that there is something greater that is worth worshiping is one thing Christians and neo-Pagans have in common, and it's a great place to start a conversation. After all, this modern longing is no different from the ancient pagan desire to worship the gods and spirits of this world that we read about in Scripture.

In fact, Scripture teaches that the original state of humanity is, in a sense, to be pagan—that is, to live on the land, connected to the webs and cycles of creation. In the book of Acts, we read that the apostle Paul healed a man in largely pagan Lystra, an ancient town in what is now Turkey. Because of their desire to worship the supernatural, the people in Lystra believed that Paul and his companion, Barnabas, were the gods Hermes and Zeus. Paul told them that they were mistaken in thinking that he or Barnabas was a god, but he did say that their desire to worship reflected knowledge of a living God. Paul told them that God left fingerprints all over creation by giving us "rain from heaven and crops in their seasons; he provides you with plenty of food and fills your hearts with joy" (Acts 14:17).

When he spoke to the people of Lystra, Paul did not begin with the Hebrew Scriptures they didn't know, but with the natural world around them that they did know and could see. Neo-Pagans today might also be interested to learn that before Jesus came, God gave us signs of his goodness and mercy in creation. Pagans both ancient and modern have recognized this. Their desire to worship and to protect the created order is a good one, perhaps even God-given.

God's plan through Jesus is to renew the earth and all that is in it—not only human souls but the whole created order. This is exciting news for the neo-Pagan seeker who loves nature. As God through Jesus redeems us, we in turn are to help heal creation for the honor and glory of its Creator until it is redeemed once and for all when Christ returns. Just as we ourselves can experience the kingdom of God here on earth even though we will not experience it in full until heaven, the same is true for the rest of creation. We are to be stewards of nature here, but creation will not be perfected until Christ's return. As I mentioned in the previous chapter, Paul wrote in Romans 8 that creation waits and groans in anticipation of being fully redeemed. So the Wiccan appreciation for and love of nature reflect God's desire for his creation as well. How sad it is that God's plan for our earthly stewardship has been misunderstood by many inside and outside the church for millennia.

An Eye for Beauty

Throughout my research I found that neo-Pagans and Wiccans had more of an eye for seeing the Divine in the beauty of nature than some Christians do, even though Scripture is clear about how God speaks to us through his creation. Psalm 19 says,

> The heavens declare the glory of God;
> the skies proclaim the work of his hands.
> Day after day they pour forth speech;
> night after night they display knowledge.
> There is no speech or language
> where their voice is not heard.
> Their voice goes out into all the earth,
> their words to the ends of the world.
> (verses 1-4)

One woman I met while researching the book told me that as a child she loved to go to the beach because when she was there, she was struck by the vast size of the ocean and the beauty of the coast. As she continued going to the beach while growing up, she soon became so aware of God's presence, his majesty, and his might in creation that at one point she was almost afraid to go because she knew he was calling her, wooing her to come to him. And eventually she did come to him.

We must not underestimate God's ability to speak to his children through the wind and the waves. Beauty in nature can draw people to God, and natural beauty certainly holds great appeal for neo-Pagans. Neo-Pagans believe that the Divine is present in nature. Most would be open to hearing the Christian perspective on this topic. And when talking with neo-Pagans, don't be surprised if you learn something from them. In his prescient book *Pollution and the Death of Man*, written in the 1970s, philosopher and theologian Francis Schaeffer wrote about Christians failing to recognize the beauty of nature, making life more austere than it needs to be, thus turning tender-hearted types toward Paganism.

While lecturing at a Christian school, Schaeffer was told that across the ravine there was a "hippie community" that engaged in pagan grape stomps. Interested, Schaeffer made his way across the ravine and met with one of the leading men in the community. They talked about ecology, and he spoke of the Christian answer to life and ecology. As they spoke, the man paid Schaeffer a compliment. He told him that he was the first person from "across the ravine" who had ever seen the place where they did indeed have pagan grape stomps. Schaeffer was also shown the pagan image that was at the center of their rites. The man then pointed to the Christian school and said, "Look at that. Isn't that ugly?" Schaeffer wrote,

> And it was! I could not deny it. It was an ugly building, without even trees around it.
>
> It was then that I realized what a poor situation this was. When I stood on Christian ground and looked at the Bohemian people's place, it was beautiful. They had even gone to the trouble of running their electric cables under the level of the trees so that they couldn't be seen. Then I stood on pagan ground and looked at the Christian community and saw ugliness. Here you have a Christianity that is failing to take into account man's responsibility and proper relationship to nature.[4]

God did not create us to live at odds with the creation, to ignore, subdue, and destroy it as so many in the church have done. Creation bears testimony to God! To do anything other than care for it grieves him.

TRUE PAGANISM

While it is important to realize that not everything about Paganism is bad, we must keep in mind what Paganism lacks. Neo-Paganism on its own, without any Christian notions of right and wrong, probably would not appeal to many practicing neo-Pagans today. Yet because they are steeped in a culture of Christianity, they are likely unaware of how many Judeo-Christian values they borrow. If we want true Paganism, to be intellectually honest about it, we have to strip away from it any elements of Christianity.

Ancient pagan religions were fatalistic—life was cheap and people lived at the mercy of the gods. The culture of caring came about as a result of the gospel message. Hospitals, orphanages, almshouses, and asylums for the blind, deaf, and dumb were outgrowths of the Christian virtue of charity. Such a culture of helping did not exist on a grand scale in the ancient pagan world. We began to value human life more after Christ came because he dignified our earthly bodies by taking on human flesh. He taught that all life has dignity because we are made in the image of God, the ancient Christian doctrine of *Imageo Deo.*

Without God, who is perfectly good, there are no absolutes, no standards by which to measure what is just or unjust. The neo-Paganism that is practiced today borrows the Christian values of right and wrong. Wiccan women are upset at the treatment of other women in history, but on what do they base their anger? According to Paganism, it is every man for himself; no woman is better than a tree or the grass on which she walks. Why should we afford any special treatment to human life at all—unless God commands it?

G. K. Chesterton was writing about this at the beginning of the twentieth century when neo-Paganism was just emerging. The "reassertors of the pagan ideal,"[5] as he called them, ignored these definite human discoveries in the moral world that were embodied in the life of Christ. The "reassertors" then and the neo-Pagans now try to have it both ways: Paganism with Christian virtues.

Chesterton notes that Christianity came after paganism and stated, "[If] the Pagan ideal will be the ultimate good of man…we must at least ask…why it was that man actually found…ultimate good on earth under the stars [i.e. paganism], and threw it away again."[6]

In other words, if paganism had been so great, why did the ideas of a peaceful Man from a poor region in the backwater of the Roman Empire, whose followers were a ragtag band of uneducated fishermen and laborers, appeal so much to the ancient pagans, the proud Romans? Perhaps it had to do with the dignity Jesus afforded women, who had known no such dignity in Greek or Roman civilization. Or the love and mercy he showed to all regardless of background. And the forgiveness he offered those who believed. Chesterton argued that the pagan virtues of reason and focus on self were tried and found wanting: "Mankind has discovered that reason does not lead to sanity. We cannot go back to an ideal of pride and enjoyment. For mankind has discovered that pride does not lead to enjoyment."[7]

A woman knows that unchecked pride and unbridled desire for enjoyment from a man can result in rape. A man knows that trying to rationalize his pain over what he has done will lead not to his comfort but to his torment. There is a better way, and it is not in waiting for the effects of karma to play themselves out or in worshiping some idealized female deity that is really ourselves dressed up in divine clothing but still subject to human flaws and shortcomings.

"If we do revive and pursue the pagan ideal of a simple and rational self-completion we shall end—where Paganism ended," says Chesterton. "I do not mean we shall end in destruction. I mean that we shall end in Christianity."[8]

Stay Humble

While we have seen that Wicca is another attempt to be satisfied with less than God, we must not pass judgment too quickly. How many Christians are daily satisfied with less than God? I know that I often am! C. S. Lewis said that infinite joy is offered to us in a relationship with God. Worshiping the created and anything other than God is "like an ignorant child who wants to go on making mud pies in a slum because he cannot imagine what is meant by the offer of a holiday at the sea. We are far too easily pleased."[9]

What we have here on earth is temporal, a mere reflection of what is to come. We have all heard of rich people who have everything they could want and are still unhappy. Yet we persist in our pursuit of earthly riches, don't we? We think that if we can just see Mount Everest, our quest for natural beauty and majesty will be satiated, or if we can just see Michelangelo's paintings in the Sistine Chapel in the Vatican, our longing to see the best artwork will be met. If we can just find a spouse; get into the right college; have children; find fame, wealth, or the perfect job, we'll be complete. The list could go on. We know from experience that this isn't true even as we chase after these things. Such things enrich our lives, but we are always left wanting more. Why is this? C. S. Lewis wrote,

The books or the music in which we thought the beauty was located will betray us if we trust to them; it was not *in* them, it only came *through* them, and what came through them was longing....

For they are not the thing itself; they are only the scent of a flower we have not found, the echo of a tune we have not heard, news from a country we have never yet visited.[10]

We are created to be in relation with God, and only he can satisfy our longings. Christians must be careful not to pass judgment on Wiccans and neo-Pagans who worship gods and goddesses, for we have our own idols when we think we will be fulfilled by anything less than God.

DANIEL: A GOOD ROLE MODEL

I have long thought that, like the apostle Paul, Daniel in the Bible serves as an excellent role model for Christians by showing us how to respond to Wicca with the right attitude and approach.

Around 605 BC, Babylon's King Nebuchadnezzar sacked Jerusalem and carried back to Babylon the spoils of his conquest, including items from the temple of God, to put in the temple erected to his pagan gods.

Daniel and several other young Israelites were summoned to live at the king's palace for three years and learn the language and literature of Babylon. This meant not only studying pagan literature but learning about their pagan religion and living among pagans. In addition, Nebuchadnezzar named Daniel the chief of magicians, enchanters, astrologers, and diviners, a man who had "the spirit of the holy gods...in him" (Daniel 4:8). Daniel was asked to eat Babylonian food, which would have violated his strict

Jewish dietary laws. So what did Daniel do? Did he sneer at their worship practices and tell them they were all going to hell? No, he resolved to abstain from the royal food and drink and not defile himself. When the administrators charged with his health voiced concern that he would fare worse than the others who consumed the royal food, he asked them to let him and three of his friends eat this way for ten days, trusting that God would provide for his health. Sure enough, after ten days on a stricter diet than the others, Daniel and his three friends looked better nourished than those who had consumed the royal food and drink.

Did God look down on Daniel for rubbing shoulders with the pagans and filling his mind with their literature? No! God *increased* the Israelites' knowledge and understanding of the pagan literature and learning. God also enabled Daniel to understand visions and dreams of all kinds.

Daniel also intervened to save the lives of other magicians, sorcerers, and astronomers in Babylon after the king ordered their execution for their inability to interpret his dreams. (The men and women who were party to the witch trials in the Middle Ages would have done well to remind themselves of Daniel. A lot of tragedy could have been averted.) Daniel petitioned the king's servant to spare the lives of the "wise men." Then Daniel went before the king, who regarded him as one of these "wise men," and said, "No wise man, enchanter, magician or diviner can explain to the king the mystery he has asked about, but there is a God in heaven who reveals mysteries" (Daniel 2:27-28). With God's help, Daniel went on to interpret Nebuchadnezzar's dream and gave glory to God as he did it. The king was so moved that he bowed down to worship Daniel's God.

Daniel was surrounded by forbidden magical practices, and he studied pagan literature, yet he never invoked any spiritual force other than God. By becoming familiar with this pagan culture, Daniel prepared himself to reveal the true living God to the Babylonians. And he was in Babylon for a long time. Daniel was called to Nebuchadnezzar's court in 607 BC, and Cyrus became king in 539 BC, which means that Daniel lived among pagans for sixty-eight years.

As Daniel's story shows us, it is important for Christians to be firm in our beliefs yet humble and meek in our treatment of others who disagree with us. The desire of Pagans to worship something greater than themselves, their love of nature, and their desire for community provides great common ground between Christians and Pagans. Too often we as Christians let matters of doctrine and belief separate us from others rather than allowing the humanity we have in common with every other person on earth to unite us. Alison's advice to fellow Christians was to live out your faith rather than preach it, so you earn the right to be heard. And listen for a long time before you speak.

LIVING WATER

The goal of Starhawk and the Living River is to bring attention to the worldwide issue of access to clean water. It is their belief that access to water is every human's right. The night I watched them chant, "We will never, never lose our way to the well of liberty…" I thought of the living water—the promise of liberty—that Jesus offered to a woman at a well two thousand years ago. She'd had five husbands, was a Samaritan outcast from Jewish society, and a woman, whom Hebrew men considered beneath them. As she drew water from the well, Jesus told her that he had *living* water for her—that whoever drank this living water would never thirst again (see John 4:14).

Jesus also discussed with her everything she had ever done. That would be an unpleasant discussion for most of us, for we all have done and thought things we don't care to share with anyone else! This Samaritan woman certainly had reason to be ashamed about talking to a Jew because she had not only had five husbands but was living with a man who was not her husband. Yet the attitude Jesus displayed toward her must have been gentle, kind, and loving because she ran back to her town and joyfully reported that Jesus had told her everything she had ever done. It had been a joyous conversation! How many of us could say that a discussion about our every deed and thought, good and bad, would be joyous?

But Jesus made her feel safe; his living water quenched her soul thirst. And that is what I believe Starhawk and her band of Pagan activists hope to bring to others—a living river to quench soul thirst. They are onto something, but they cast *themselves* and creation as the living water rather than the One who can redeem us all and provide "water...[that] will become...a spring of water welling up to eternal life" (John 4:14). Many Wiccans and Pagans yearn to provide liberty for the captives and water for the poor, yet history shows that neither men nor women, nor a pagan god or goddess, can do this for humankind. What pagan deity came down from heaven and took on the human form of a baby to provide living water for our souls? But there is Someone who did, and he has shown that he speaks to the Pagans and bids them come to him, the Source of that living water.

WISE MEN

The wise men described in Matthew's gospel are thought to be pagan astrologers from the East who saw a star and knew it led to a king. Matthew tells us that when the wise men arrived in Jerusalem, they asked, "Where is the one who has been born king of the Jews? We saw his star in the east and have come to worship him" (Matthew 2:2).

Interestingly, the word *Wicca* can be translated "wise one." Wiccans themselves could be called wise men or wise women. And the wise men were also known as "the Magi," which comes from the Latin root *mag* meaning "sorcerer" or "magician."

The incredible truth is that among the first people to be drawn to Jesus—God made flesh, the Messiah—were none other than Gentile, pagan magicians. They came because God drew them to himself through creation, a star.

"The heavens declare the glory of God; the skies proclaim the work of his hands. Day after day they pour forth speech; night after night they display knowledge..." (Psalm 19:1-2).

Today's Pagans might have similar experiences as the wise men. They might see something in nature or read something that causes them to consider Christ. The Christian's role is then to come alongside them, as Paul did in Acts, and answer questions to help fill in any gaps in their understanding. Perhaps, by the Holy Spirit, this can lead to their salvation.

So as Wicca grows in popularity in the West, Christians need not fear. The Scriptures show that God has been drawing pagans to himself for millennia. He is so familiar with the yearnings of pagans that he called pagan magicians to visit the Christ child, who was God in human flesh.

By his Spirit may we follow his example so that today's wise men and women will continue to seek and find him.

AFTERWORD

As I said in the preface to this book, it is never easy to be an outsider writing about other people's spirituality. The spiritual teaching I received growing up taught me to have nothing to do with witchcraft and pagan religions. Yet here I faced a dilemma: I wanted to get to know the people who practiced this spirituality. So looking to Daniel and Paul as my role models, I needed to become familiar with these religions.

When I first encountered Wicca, I am ashamed to say that I allowed myself to laugh at followers of the Craft—to scoff at their beliefs and at them as human beings. In light of the long history of Christians acting this way, I quickly realized this was the wrong approach. How could I scoff at the beliefs of Wiccans without spending time with them or reading their literature in depth?

My fear in writing this book was that the believing Christians whom I wanted to read it would assume, as I did, they already know all there is to know about Wiccans or that they would feel they should steer clear of all things occultish, including learning anything about Wicca. Also, I wanted the book to point out ways the church has not met the spiritual needs of seekers, but I knew some Christians would be uncomfortable with such an analysis. For those of you who have read to this point, I am very grateful.

I must admit that one of the more upsetting things in my journalistic history is that several of my early articles about Wicca were condescending in tone, subject to the whims of editors and the tyranny of the deadline. I was, in fact, expected to look down on Wicca. I remember being severely chastised in an editorial meeting for writing a fairly balanced article about

Wicca in a conservative publication. In this book I have tried to treat Wicca honorably and fairly.

Writing this book was a journey that opened my eyes. I hope yours have been opened as well. What I have conveyed here are my observations from a world little traveled by the rest of America. I wrote this book not as an academic or a theologian, but as a journalist passing on her insights about this Western spiritual phenomenon from a Christian perspective.

For a year I traveled across the United States interviewing people and asking them questions about Wicca, neo-Paganism, and Christianity. This research was done with the help of a grant from the Phillips Foundation in the form of a journalism fellowship. I not only wanted to hear the stories of ordinary people, but I wanted to understand their worldviews and why they claimed to have found meaning in Wicca or other Pagan beliefs. As with any spirituality, there are the superstars—the well-known practitioners. I interviewed some of them, but my main goal was to speak with regular people who had sought out this spirituality. I met people in person and over the telephone. When neither of these worked, I contacted them through e-mail. Most names were changed to protect the identity of those I interviewed.

My job as a reporter was to ask questions and write my story. The more people I talked with, though, the more I was flooded with personal insights. That is the great thing about journalism—you get paid (although usually not very much) to talk to interesting people you would never normally encounter. These people in turn can have a significant impact on your life.

As I traveled I tried to be open-minded and fair in my interviews. My research soon revealed an intriguing critique of my own faith community. I was amazed that frustration with the Christian church came up again and again as I interviewed people. I wondered, though, what sort of gospel these people had encountered and whether their rejection of Christianity was based on a rejection of the message of Jesus of Nazareth, a distorted view of his teachings, or other reasons altogether. I soon discovered the answer to that question: No one disliked Jesus. They only disliked those who profess to be his messengers! It is a shame that some Christians have given Christianity a bad name.

My hope in writing this book is that I have equipped you with helpful knowledge so that if a Wiccan or neo-Pagan should cross your path in life, you will be able to demonstrate the understanding, love, and acceptance that Jesus has for them and will be able to engage them in constructive dialogue, sharing with them the hope of the gospel. If you are Wiccan and are fleeing Christianity or have never really considered it in the first place, I hope you will give the message of Jesus of Nazareth a serious look.

Appendix

Not in Kansas Anymore

R eaders and movie lovers might be surprised to learn that one of the best-selling children's books of all time, *The Wizard of Oz* by L. Frank Baum, fits right in with the worldview of modern Pagans. Far ahead of its time, the book was based on feminist ideas, the myth of matriarchal prehistory, and the hope of a social utopia.

Baum was married to Maud Gage, daughter of early feminist activist and suffrage activist Matilda Joslyn Gage. Matilda Gage made a name for herself when she published the three-volume *History of Woman Suffrage* (1881–1889) with Susan B. Anthony and Elizabeth Cady Stanton. Gage's ideas had a profound influence on her son-in-law, and his books for children reflected many of her radical ideas. Pulitzer Prize–winner Alison Lurie writes:

> Among Matilda Gage's striking and original views was her belief in a prehistoric matriarchal society, "The Matriarchate." In *Woman, Church, and State* (1895), partly written when she was living in Chicago with Baum and his family, she declared that all ancient communities had been ruled by women: "A form of society existed at an early age known as the Matriarchate or Mother-rule. Under the Matriarchate, except as son and inferior, man was not recognized in either of these great institutions, family, state or church. A father and husband as such, had no place either in the social, political or religious scheme; woman was ruler in each."[1]

In the land of Oz, men were portrayed as weak. The Wizard of Oz, who ran the Emerald City, turned out to be a fraud, an incompetent with no magical powers at all. The Scarecrow, who lacked a brain, could feel but not think; the Tin Man had no heart; and the Cowardly Lion lacked courage. Only through the ingenuity of Dorothy, the female heroine, did they acquire these things. And witches, good and bad, ruled Oz.

Gage's views on witches had a formative effect not only on Baum but on the mid-twentieth-century revival of Paganism and witchcraft. Gage's view, shared by some Wiccans today, was that under the tyranny of patriarchal rule, some women continued to observe the beliefs and rituals of earlier times. The witches of the late medieval and early modern age were pagan priestesses, skilled in healing. Gage was also against racial and ethnic prejudice. You can also see this in Baum's books, which are filled with people who are different from others.

Not unlike many young women today, Gage embraced the idea of a peaceful society ruled by women. She had lived through the brutal and bloody Civil War and saw what devastation men can wreak on one another. It is no wonder she thought the world would be a better place if women ruled it. They had never had a chance in her lifetime to do much of anything, except marry and have children. Her ideal was for women to have power over men, and she saw the legendary witches of old as the great arbiters of that power.

Women today who have been mistreated by men or have seen men mistreat other women often embrace Wicca and its political views for the same reasons Matilda Gage and Frank Baum protested social ills one hundred years ago.

Notes

Preface

1. Barbara Sciacca, "Honoring Our Bodies, Honoring Our Lives," *Woman of Power* 19 (winter 1991): 63, quoted and paraphrased from Viola Larson, "Wicca: Searching for Identity, Meaning, and Community in the Lonely Shadows of Witchcraft," *TruthQuest Journal* 2, no. 3 (autumn 1998), posted on *Naming the Grace,* www.naminggrace.org/id38_m.htm.

2. See Kathryn Fuller, Covenant of the Goddess, "Wiccan/Pagan Poll Final Results," press release, October 7, 2000, www.cog.org/cogpoll_final.html.

3. See Helen A. Berger, *A Community of Witches: Contemporary Neo-Paganism and Witchcraft in the United States* (Columbia, SC: University of South Carolina Press, 1999), 9.

4. See Berger, *A Community of Witches,* 10.

Chapter 1

1. See Phyllis Curott, *Witch Crafting: A Spiritual Guide to Making Magic* (New York: Broadway, 2001), 1.

2. Anne Niven, interview by Keith Olbermann, *Countdown with Keith Olbermann,* MSNBC, June 9, 2003.

3. Aidan Kelly, "Aporrtheton No. 1: To the New Witch," March 1973, quoted in Margot Adler, *Drawing Down the Moon: Witches, Druids, Goddess-Worshippers, and Other Pagans in America Today* (New York: Penguin, 1979), 170.

4. The Barna Group, "Americans Draw Theological Beliefs from Diverse Points of View," *The Barna Update,* October 8, 2002, www.barna.org. Used by permission.

5. Starhawk (speech, Women's Words Women's Power Writer Series, Sonoma State University, Rohnert Park, CA, March 13, 2002).

6. Starhawk (speech, Sonoma State, March 13, 2002).

7. Curott, *Witch Crafting,* 54.

8. See Curott, *Witch Crafting,* 6-7.

9. See Scott Cunningham, *The Truth About Witchcraft Today* (St. Paul, MN: Llewellyn, 1988), 115-18.

10. Cable Neuhaus, "Salem's Official Witch, Laurie Cabot, Finds Grave Errors in Eastwick," *People,* June 29, 1987, 52.

11. Laurie Cabot, quoted in Neuhaus, "Salem's Official Witch," 52.

12. See Neuhaus, "Salem's Official Witch," 52.

13. Associated Press, " 'Witch' Descendants Urge State to Exonerate Ancestors," *Washington Times,* May 28, 2001.

Chapter 2

1. Matthew Fox (speech, Techno Cosmic Mass, Oakland, California, March 2003).

2. George Gallup and D. Michael Lindsay, *The Gallup Guide: Reality Check for 21st Century Churches* (Washington, DC: Gallup Organization, 2002), quoted in Helen T. Gray, "Book Introduces the Soul-Searching Survey," *Tallahassee Democrat,* March 1, 2003.

3. Os Guinness, *The Dust of Death* (Downers Grove, IL: InterVarsity, 1973), 281.

4. Charles Manson, quoted in David Felton and David Dalton, "Year of the Fork, Night of the Hunter," *Rolling Stone,* June 25, 1970, www.charliemanson.com/rolling-stone-1.htm.

5. Jonathan Rauch, "Let It Be," *Atlantic Monthly,* May 2003, www.theatlantic.com/issues/2003/05/rauch.htm.

Chapter 3

1. See David Rieff, "Multiculturalism's Silent Partner," *Harper's,* August 1993, 62, 72.

2. Jan Ferris Heenan, "Divination=Divine Sales," *Publishers Weekly,* May 21, 2001, www.publishersweekly.com.

3. Cate Tiernan, quoted in "Biographical Essay," *Authors and Artists for Young Adults* 49 (2003), www.firefairy.eve7k.com/author/ct_galenet.php.

4. Lauren F. Winner, "Nurturing Today's Teen Spirit," *Publishers Weekly,* March 12, 2001, 30.

5. The Barna Group, "More Americans Are Seeking Net-Based Faith Experiences," *The Barna Update,* May 21, 2001, www.barna.org. Used by permission.

6. Pat Devin, "An Interview with Pat Devin," Cyberwitch.com, 1998, in Brooks Alexander, *Witchcraft Goes Mainstream: Uncovering Its Alarming Impact on You and Your Family* (Eugene, OR: Harvest House, 2004), 94-95.

7. According to Reclaiming's promotional materials, after the publication of her book *The Spiral Dance* in 1979, Starhawk began to teach classes on ritual work with a friend in the San Francisco Bay area. The classes grew in popularity and soon students were branching off to

teach others. They called themselves the Reclaiming Collective: a group committed to neo-Pagan witchcraft, feminism, nonviolence, no formal hierarchy, and reverence for the earth. In 1982 members of the collective protested a proposed local nuclear power plant. Soon thereafter began a trend of Reclaiming witches participating in political action. In the early 1990s, the IRS awarded Reclaiming tax-exempt status as a nonprofit religious organization. Today, thousands of men and women might call themselves Reclaiming witches. It is its own form of witchcraft. Reclaiming publishes a newsletter, holds public rituals on the Witches' sabbaths, offers classes and ritual training and holds weeklong witchcraft training retreats—Witch Camps. Participants in the weeklong camps "share in a week of earth based spirituality and magic." See also Jody Logan and Patti Martin, "Reclaiming: History, Structure, and the Future," *Reclaiming* (Winter 1995), www.reclaiming.org/about/origins/history-loganymartin.html.

8. Wicca 101 course description, Witches' Voice Web site, www .witchvox.com/vn/vn_detail/dt_ev.html?a=usva&id=36246, accessed May 23, 2005.

Chapter 4

1. Margot Adler (speech, Women of Wisdom Spirituality Conference, Seattle Unity Church, Seattle, Washington, February 16, 2002).

2. Carol Christ, "Religion and the Feminist Movement," (speech, Harvard Divinity School, November 2002). Her remarks are also published in Ann Braude, ed., *Transforming the Faith of Our Fathers: Women Who Changed American Religion* (New York: Palgrave Macmillan, 2004), 97-114.

3. Carol Christ, *Rebirth of the Goddess: Finding Meaning in Feminist Spirituality* (New York: Routledge, 1997), xiii.

4. See Cynthia Eller, *Living in the Lap of the Goddess: The Feminist Spirituality Movement in America* (Boston: Beacon Press, 1993), 3.

5. See Os Guinness, *The Dust of Death* (Downers Grove, IL: Inter Varsity, 1973), 281.

6. See Margot Adler, *Drawing Down the Moon: Witches, Druids, Goddess-Worshippers, and Other Pagans in American Today* (New York: Penguin, 1979), 45-46.

7. Other sources for the matriarchal myth include Starhawk, *The Spiral Dance: A Rebirth of the Ancient Religion of the Great Goddess* (San Francisco: HarperSanFrancisco, 1999), 29, 31, 32; Raymond Buckland, *Wicca for Life: The Way of the Craft–From Birth to Summerland* (New York: Citadel Press, 2001), 7, 10.

8. Albert Gore, *Earth in the Balance: Healing the Global Environment* (New York: Houghton Mifflin, 1992), 260.

9. Margot Adler, "A Time for Truth," www.beliefnet.com/story/40/story_4007.html. Accessed April 8, 2005.

10. Adler, "Time for Truth."

11. Jenny Gibbons, "Recent Developments in the Study of the Great European Witch Hunt," *The Pomegranate: A New Journal of Neopagan Thought* 5 (Summer 1998).

12. Gibbons, "Recent Developments."

13. Robin Briggs, *Witches and Neighbors: The Social and Cultural Context of European Witchcraft* (New York: Penguin, 1996), 5, 8, 260.

14. Starhawk, "Letters to the Editor," *The Atlantic Monthly*, April 2001, 12.

15. See Ronald Hutton, *The Triumph of the Moon: A History of Modern Pagan Witchcraft* (Oxford: Oxford University Press, 1999), 136.

16. See Hutton, *Triumph of the Moon,* 138.

17. See Olivia Vlahos, "The Goddess That Failed," *First Things* 28 (December 1992): 13.

18. See Margaret Alice Murray, *Witch Cult in Western Europe: A Study in Anthropology* (Oxford: Clarendon, 1921), 12.

19. See Murray, *Witch Cult,* 47, 60.

20. See Murray, *Witch Cult,* 153-56.

21. See Murray, *Witch Cult,* 50-59.

22. See Jack L. Bracelin, *Gerald Gardner: Witch* (London: Octagon, 1960), in Philip G. Davis, *Goddess Unmasked: The Rise of Neopagan Feminist Spirituality* (Dallas: Spence Publishing, 1998), 332.

23. See Hutton, *Triumph of the Moon,* 206.

24. See Adler, *Drawing Down the Moon,* 46.

25. Doreen Valiente, *Rebirth of Witchcraft* (Custer, WA: Phoenix, 1989), 51-52, in Davis, *Goddess Unmasked,* 334.

26. Phyllis Curott, *Witch Crafting: A Spiritual Guide to Making Magic* (New York: Broadway, 2002), 23.

27. See Patricia Crowther, "The Day I Met Aleister Crowley," *Prediction* 36, no. 11 (November 1970): 14; Francis King, *Ritual Magic in England: 1887 to the Present Day* (London: Spearman, n.d.), 176-81; in Hutton, *Triumph of the Moon,* 218.

28. See Aleister Crowley, *The Law Is for All* (Scottsdale, AZ: New Falcon, 1991), 114.

29. See Hutton, *Triumph of the Moon,* 179.

30. See Hutton, *Triumph of the Moon,* 229.

31. See Davis, *Goddess Unmasked,* 336-37.

32. Antoinette LaFarge and Robert Allen, "The Best of the Beast: How Do You Sort the Gold from the Dross in Aleister Crowley's Work?" *Gnosis* 24 (summer 1992): 33-35, quoted in Davis, *Goddess Unmasked,* 254.

33. Jesus taught that God is spirit (John 4:24). God is not to be represented as male or female (Exodus 20:4; Deuteronomy 4:16).

34. Adler, Women of Wisdom Spirituality Conference.

35. Peggy Orenstein, "Mourning My Miscarriage," *New York Times Magazine,* April 21, 2002, 38, 40.

36. Orenstein, "Mourning My Miscarriage," 41.

37. Adler, Women of Wisdom Spirituality Conference.

38. Roberta Hestenes, "Religion and the Feminist Movement" (speech, Harvard Divinity School, November 2002). Taken from author's notes.

Chapter 5

1. Mary Daly, "Religion and the Feminist Movement" (speech, Harvard Divinity School, November 2002), quoted in Mark Oppenheimer, "God and Women at Harvard at a Religion Conference: The Feminist Faithful Tread Carefully," *Boston Globe,* November 24, 2002.

2. Jean Kilbourne, *Deadly Persuasion: Why Women and Girls Must Fight the Addictive Power of Advertising* (New York: Free Press, 1999), 133.

3. Kilbourne, *Deadly Persuasion,* 132-33.

4. Karen Kersting, "Driving Teen Egos—and Buying—Through 'Branding,' " *Monitor on Psychology* 35, no. 6 (June 2004): 60.

5. Kilbourne, *Deadly Persuasion,* 143.

6. Kilbourne, *Deadly Persuasion,* 110.

7. Ann Belford Ulanov, "The Witch Archetype" (lecture, Analytical Psychology Club, New York, November 17, 1976); *Quadrant* 10, no. 1 (1977): 5-22, quoted in Margot Adler, *Drawing Down the Moon: Witches, Druids, Goddess-Worshippers, and Other Pagans in American Today* (New York: Penguin, 1979), 41.

8. Mardi Keyes, personal conversation, May 31, 2005.

9. See Rodney Stark, *The Rise of Christianity: A Sociologist Reconsiders History* (Princeton: Princeton University Press, 1996), 95, 102-4, 118.

10. See Catherine of Siena, *Catherine of Siena: The Dialogue,* trans. Suzanne Noffke (New York: Paulist, 1980), 3-7.

11. Teresa of Ávila, *The Life of Saint Teresa of Ávila by Herself* (New York: Penguin Classics, 1957), 11, 14.

12. Patricia C. McKissack and Frederick McKissack, *Sojourner Truth: Ain't I a Woman* (New York: Scholastic, 1992), 111-14.

13. Christabel Pankhurst, *Christian,* October 21, 1926, 24, quoted in Timothy Larsen, *Christabel Pankhurst: Fundamentalism and Feminism in Coalition* (Woodbridge, Suffolk: Boydell Press, 2002), 117.

14. See Larsen, *Christabel Pankhurst,* 109-10.

Chapter 6

1. The Barna Group, "New Barna Book Provides Insight into Real Teens," *The Barna Update,* October 8, 2001, www.barna.org. Used by permission.

2. See Helen A. Berger, Evan A. Leach, and Leigh S. Shaffer, "Voices from the Pagan Census: A National Survey of Witches and Neo-Pagans in the United States (Columbia, SC: University of South Carolina Press, 2003), 216.

3. See Matthew Nisbet, "Why Are We Pushing Witchcraft on Teen-Age Girls Instead of Promoting Science and Math?" *Buffalo News,* November 7, 1998.

4. Ruth La Ferla, "Like Magic, Witchcraft Charms Teenagers," *New York Times,* February 13, 2000.

5. La Ferla, "Like Magic, Witchcraft Charms Teenagers."

Chapter 7

1. David Abel, "Back to Nature Paganism Growing in Popularity on Nation's Campuses," *Boston Globe,* October 31, 2000.

2. Abel, "Back to Nature Paganism."

3. Lehigh University Chaplain's Office, "Religious Holidays: Policy and Calendar," spring 2005, www.lehigh.edu/~incha/holidays.html.

4. Mark Noll, "The Evangelical Mind Today," *First Things* 146 (October 2004): 38-39.

5. Noll, "Evangelical Mind," 39.

6. John R. W. Stott, *Christian Mission in the Modern World: What the Church Should Be Doing Now* (Downers Grove, IL: InterVarsity, 1975), 72.

Chapter 8

1. Christine Hoff Kraemer, "Pagans and Christians: Toward a Reconciliation of Opposites," Trinity United Methodist Church, 2001, www.tumc.org.

2. Flier, "The Goddess Returns to Ghost Ranch," quoted in Donna F. G. Hailson and Karelynne Gerber, "Cooking Up Gotterdamerung: Radical Feminist Worship Substitutes Self for God," *Theology Matters* 4, no. 4 (July/August 1998): 4.

3. Catherine Edwards, "Wicca Infiltrates the Church," *Insight,* December 6, 1999, 16.

4. See Edwards, "Wicca Infiltrates the Church," 16.

5. Edwards, "Wicca Infiltrates the Church," 16.

6. Sue Monk Kidd, *The Dance of the Dissident Daughter: A Woman's Journey from the Christian Tradition to the Sacred Feminine* (San Francisco: HarperSanFrancisco, 1996), 34.

7. Edwards, "Wicca Infiltrates the Church," 15.

8. John R. W. Stott, *Christian Mission in the Modern World: What the Church Should Be Doing Now* (Downers Grove, IL: InterVarsity, 1975), 71.

9. Grove Harris, "Yes, Dorothy, Witchcamp Is Probably Coming to Kansas," *Spirituality and Health,* summer 2000, 21.

10. Rosemari G. Sullivan, "Resources for Jubilee," The Seventy-Third General Convention of the Episcopal Church, 2000.

11. Paul G. Heibert, "The Flaw of the Excluded Middle," *Missiology* 10, no. 1 (January 1982): 35-47, in George G. Hunter III, *The Celtic Way of Evangelism: How Christianity Can Reach the West...Again* (Nashville: Abingdon, 2000), 31.

12. Hunter, *Celtic Way of Evangelism,* 32.

13. Esther de Waal, *The Celtic Way of Prayer* (New York: Doubleday, 1997), 30-31.

Chapter 9

1. "Principles of Unity," Reclaiming Collective Annual Retreat, November 8, 1997, www.reclaiming.org/about/directions/unity.html.

2. Starhawk, *Dreaming the Dark: Magic, Sex and Politics* (Boston: Beacon Press, 1997), xxv.

3. Starhawk, *Dreaming the Dark*, 180.

4. Starhawk, *Webs of Power: Notes from the Global Uprising* (Gabriola Island, B. C.: New Society, 2002), 162.

5. Starhawk, *Webs of Power*, 163.

6. Martin Heidegger, *The Question of Being* (New York: Twayne, 1958), 19.

7. Simone Weil, *The Need for Roots: Prelude to a Declaration of Duties Towards Mankind* (New York: Routledge, 1952), 9.

8. Paraphrased and quoted from Alan Thein Durning, *This Place on Earth: Home and the Practice of Permanence* (Seattle: Sasquatch Books, 1996), 3-4.

9. Phillip Jenkins, "The Next Christianity," *Atlantic Monthly* 209, no. 3 (October 2002), www.theatlantic.com/issues/2002/10/jenkins.htm.

10. Information about A Rocha is from www.en.arocha.org.

11. David Bookless, "Between the Rock and a Hard Place: The Developing Work of A Rocha," *Ecotheology* 7, no. 2 (January 2003): 219.

12. David Bookless, correspondence with author, March 31, 2005.

Chapter 10

1. C. S. Lewis, *Surprised by Joy: The Shape of My Early Life* (Glasgow: Collins Sons, 1955), 12.

2. C. S. Lewis, *The Weight of Glory and Other Addresses* (New York: Macmillan, 1949), 12.

3. John Piper, *Seeing and Savoring Jesus Christ* (Wheaton, IL: Crossway, 2004), 14.

4. Francis Schaeffer and Udo Middleman, *Pollution and the Death of Man: The Christian View of Ecology* (Wheaton, IL: Crossway, 1970), 42-43.
5. Gilbert K. Chesterton, *Heretics* (New York: John Lane, 1905), 169.
6. Chesterton, *Heretics,* 156.
7. Chesterton, *Heretics,* 169-70.
8. Chesterton, *Heretics,* 170.
9. Lewis, *Weight of Glory,* 2.
10. Lewis, *Weight of Glory,* 4-5.

Appendix

1. Alison Lurie, "The Oddness of Oz," *New York Review,* December 21, 2000, 16.

Glossary

Following is a glossary of terms that are commonly used within neo-Paganism. Understanding these terms will help you become familiar with the language used in neo-Pagan circles. Please refer to this list often as you read the book.

ankh. An ancient Egyptian symbol resembling a cross with a loop at the top. Mythological gods and goddesses are seen carrying it in Egyptian works of art. The ankh is used by many Wiccans in spells and rituals involving health, fertility, and divination.

athame. A ritual knife or ceremonial dagger used by Wiccans in some rites to direct natural energy from within the body to the outside world.

Beltane festival. The celebration of one of the eight annual witches sabbats celebrated on the first day of May or on the eve of the first day of May. Beltane is a time for celebrating Mother Nature and dancing around the Maypole, which is an obvious phallic fertility symbol that is placed in the "womb" of Mother Earth.

book of shadows. A personalized spiritual diary or journal of a witch's experiences; a handbook for things occultic; might contain spells, rites, and rituals.

Celtic pantheon. The gods and goddesses of the ancient Celtic peoples of Britain and Ireland. The Greek gods and goddesses would be referred to as the Greek pantheon; the gods and goddesses of the Romans, the Roman pantheon, and so on.

censer. A metal vessel with a perforated lid that is used as an incense burner in many Wiccan rituals.

ceremonial magic. The working of magic through elaborate magical rituals. By precisely performing a ritual, the practitioner is supposed to be able to control spiritual entities or powers of nature or intensify his or her own psychic powers to affect the desired result.

cone of power. A name for the "cone" of psychic powered energy that witches claim to conjure up from the earth into themselves. The goal is to visualize energy in the form of a spiral rising from the earth into the body, and then direct it toward a specific goal or task.

coven. A group of people who convene for religious, magic, or psychic purposes; usually refers to a meeting of witches. Some Wiccan covens are very formal while others are informal, almost social gatherings.

the Craft. A shorthand way to refer to Wicca or modern witchcraft.

craft name. A new name witches choose for themselves upon initiation into witchcraft.

crone. A wise older woman in the Wiccan community. To Wiccans, the crone represents maturity and wisdom. The Mother Goddess is also said to have three roles or phases that correspond to the seasons of life: maiden, mother, and crone.

croning ritual. A ritual in which Wiccans honor the passage of a woman into the crone phase of life.

Dianic. Feminist witchcraft; Dianic covens emphasize or sometimes exclusively worship the Mother Goddess. Some of these covens allow men to join while others are only for women.

divination. The act or practice of trying to foretell the future or explore the unknown by occult means.

Druid. Member of a Celtic religious order of priests, soothsayers, judges, and poets in ancient Britain and Ireland. Druids today claim to engage in the same practices and beliefs as their ancient counterparts.

esbats. Wiccan celebrations centered on the lunar cycles.

evangelical. Since the word *evangel* means "the gospel" or "good news" of the New Testament, *evangelical* means "according to the teaching of the gospel or New Testament." The word commonly refers to churches that emphasize salvation by faith alone, not by adding good works or sacraments to faith.

Gardnerian witchcraft. The most well known of Wiccan traditions, named after its founder, Gerald Gardner. The Gardnerian tradition centers on the worship of the Mother Goddess and the Horned God. Strict followers of this tradition worship nude and practice ritual scourging to raise magical power. Most Wiccan traditions have their roots in Gardnerian witchcraft.

goddess. A female god worshiped as a deity with supernatural powers. Examples are Athena, Greek goddess of war; Artemis, Greek goddess of the hunt; and Aphrodite, Greek goddess of love.

(Mother) Goddess. A metaphor for the earth. Wiccans believe that Mother Goddess was present at the dawn of time and that the goddesses Wiccans worship are manifestations of the Mother Goddess. She is also known as the Triple Goddess because of her three main roles: maiden, mother, crone.

Goddess worship. A form of neo-Pagan spirituality whose practitioners worship the Mother Goddess; in America, Goddess worship is largely rooted in feminism.

herbalism. The practice of growing or dealing in herbs, especially medicinally or spiritually.

Horned God. Primary male deity experienced, invoked, and worshiped by witches. He is the consort to the Mother Goddess.

karma. From Sanskrit meaning "action," it is the universal law of cause and effect that governs reincarnation. For every action there are moral ramifications and consequences.

kitchen witch. A practical witch who is often eclectic and focuses on magic and spirituality centering around the hearth and home.

magic. An attempt or supposed ability to manipulate reality for one's own purposes and desires by invoking or employing spirits, unseen forces, and guides. In some Wiccan circles it is spelled *magick* to distinguish it from card tricks or the pulling-a-rabbit-out-of-a-hat type of magic.

mainline. Commonly refers to churches that have a well-established social position but aren't always evangelical.

metaphysical shop. A shop that sells books and paraphernalia related to the supernatural, unseen world of the occult.

monism. The belief that reality is an organic whole without any independent parts—"all is one"—and that the cosmos is pure, undifferentiated universal energy. All of life is considered to be of equal value, and everything is one vast interconnected process.

neo-Pagan. Someone who practices a modern form of earth-based spirituality incorporating nature worship through a revival of the worship of ancient gods and goddesses.

occult. Hidden, concealed from human view, mysterious. Often refers to spiritual practices.

pagan. From the Latin word *paganus,* which means "country-dweller." Generally refers to people who do not believe in Christianity or Judaism, but more specifically refers to ancient peoples who venerated nature through its worship and the worship of gods and goddesses, such as ancient Greeks, Romans, Norse peoples, or Britons.

Pagan. A shorthand version of the word "neo-Pagan"; somcone who practices a modern form of earth-based spirituality incorporating nature worship through a revival of the worship of ancient gods and goddesses.

Paganism. A modern earth-based spirituality incorporating nature worship through a revival of the worship of ancient gods and goddess.

panentheism. Belief that acknowledges that God is not equal to the earth but that all things exist in God.

pantheism. The doctrine that God is not a personality but that all laws, forces, and manifestations of the universe are God.

pentagram. A five-pointed star; a Wiccan symbol whose five points represent the five elements of air, fire, water, earth, and spirit.

psychic abilities. Either inherent abilities or powers that can be tapped into, which everyone supposedly possesses, can develop, or can access to work divination, magic, and sorcery. These abilities result in occultic or paranormal phenomena.

psychokinesis. The ability to move an object without physically touching it.

ritual. A set form or system of religious rites and ceremonies. A common Wiccan ritual, which takes place during a full moon, is called "drawing down the moon." Wiccans believe that the moon represents the Mother Goddess, and this ritual is performed to tap into her power. A man and woman (usually the coven's high priest and priestess) are required for the ceremony. The coven sits in a circle around the high priest and priestess, and the high priestess stands with her hands raised and stretched out above her head. The high priest kneels in front of her and raises his athame, or ritual knife, and calls upon the Goddess to enter the body of the high priestess. He draws a pentagram with his athame, lowers it, and sits back. The high priestess then speaks to the Goddess, but sometimes words are spoken that Wiccans claim come directly from the Goddess with the high priestess acting as a "channel" relaying the Goddess's words to the members of the coven.

runes. Letters from an alphabet, which Wiccans claim is secret and magical. Runes are carved onto ritual tools, talismans, amulets, stones, or flat wooden sticks and are used during rituals and divination.

sabbats. Eight annual Wiccan celebrations centered on the solar cycles.

Samhain. The Celtic name for Halloween; the most important of the eight sabbats celebrated by Wiccans. Wiccans believe that the "veil" separating the living from the dead is thinnest on this night, making it easier for the two to communicate.

Satanism. The worship of Satan (the being described in the Bible); Wiccans deny belief in him.

scourge. A whip or instrument for flogging that is used in certain Wiccan ceremonies.

shamanism. Religious practices of peoples (more pervasive among North Asians and Native Americans) who believe that spirits pervade the world and can be summoned by inspired priests acting as mediums.

soothsayer. Someone who claims to be able to foretell the future.

spell. A word, formula, incantation, or form of words thought to have some magical power; seemingly magical power or irresistible influence; symbolic acts performed in an altered state of consciousness in order to bring about a desired change.

syncretism. The combining or mixing of religions or religious beliefs, practices, and philosophies. This results in new or hybrid religions that are composed of diverse elements of the religions from which they are derived.

talisman. A man-made object of any shape or material that is charged by a Wiccan with magical properties and is used to bring good luck or fertility or to ward off evil spirits.

tarot cards. A deck of cards used for reading the past and the future as well as fortunes.

Threefold Law. The Wiccan belief that whatever you do will come back to you multiplied three times. For example, someone who does good will receive three times as much good in this life, and often immediately. Those who do harm to others will receive three times as much harm as they have done.

Welsh witchcraft. A Wiccan tradition in which a Welsh pantheon of gods and goddesses is worshiped.

Wicca. Neo-Pagan witchcraft practiced as a spirituality or religion. A polytheistic neo-Pagan nature religion inspired by various pre-Christian Western European beliefs, which has as its central deity the Mother Goddess and which includes the use of herbal magic and witchcraft. Linguists differ over the origin of the word's meaning. Some say *Wicca* comes from the Old English word *wic* or *weik,* which means "to bend or shape." Others say the root word is *wit* meaning "wisdom."

Wiccan Rede. The closest thing Wiccans have to a moral code: "Do what you will [and] you harm none." Wiccans believe that they are free to do whatever they want, provided no harm comes to anyone. The individual practitioner determines what it means to do no harm.

witch. Traditionally understood as a woman with supernatural powers. Neo-Pagans define witch as a male or female who practices Wicca.

witchcamp. A training retreat for witches, particularly in the Reclaiming tradition, in which participants take classes and learn about Wicca.

witchcraft. Nature-oriented, experience-based spirituality whose followers are polytheists, panentheists, and pantheists. Some believe in and invoke the Mother Goddess and her consort, the Horned God. Followers are antiauthoritarian and antidogmatic. Also called Wicca, the Craft, or Craft of the wise.

women's spirituality. Overarching term that refers to neo-Paganism and Goddess worship practiced by women with feminist sympathies.

FURTHER RESOURCES

BOOKS

Academic Resources

Berger, Helen A. *A Community of Witches: Contemporary Neo-Paganism and Witchcraft in the United States.* Columbia, SC: University of South Carolina Press, 1999.

Berger, Helen A., Evan A. Leach, and Leigh S. Shaffer. *Voices from the Pagan Census: A National Survey of Witches and Neo-Pagans in the United States.* Columbia, SC: University of South Carolina Press, 2003.

Davis, Philip G. *Goddess Unmasked: The Rise of Neo-Pagan Feminist Spirituality.* Dallas: Spence, 1999.

Eller, Cynthia. *Living in the Lap of the Goddess: The Feminist Spirituality Movement in America.* Boston: Beacon Press, 1995.

———. *The Myth of Matriarchal Prehistory: Why an Invented Past Will Not Give Women a Future.* Boston: Beacon Press, 2001.

Gimbutas, Marija A. *The Gods and Goddesses of Old Europe, 7000 to 3500 B.C.: Myths, Legends, and Cult Images.* Berkeley, CA: University of California Press, 1974.

———. *The Language of the Goddess: Unearthing the Hidden Symbols of Western Civilization.* San Francisco: HarperSanFrancisco, 1995.

Hutton, Ronald. *The Triumph of the Moon: A History of Modern Pagan Witchcraft.* Oxford: Oxford University Press, 2001.

Murray, Margaret A. *The God of the Witches.* Whitefish, MT: Kessinger, 2004.

———. *The Witch Cult in Western Europe: A Study in Anthropology.* Whitefish, MT: Kessinger, 2004.

Christian Apologetics

Barnett, Paul W. *Is the New Testament Reliable? A Look at the Historical Evidence.* Downers Grove, IL: InterVarsity, 1992.

Clark, David K., and Norman L. Geisler. *Apologetics in the New Age: A Christian Critique of Pantheism.* Eugene, OR: Wipf and Stock, 2004.

Strobel, Lee. *The Case for Christ: A Journalist's Personal Investigation of the Evidence for Jesus.* Grand Rapids: Zondervan, 2002.

Christian Commentary on Culture

Alexander, Brooks. *Witchcraft Goes Mainstream: Uncovering Its Alarming Impact on You and Your Family.* Eugene, OR: Harvest House, 2004.

Chesterton, G. K. *The Everlasting Man.* Whitefish, MT: Kessinger, 2004.

———. *Heretics.* Whitefish, MT: Kessinger, 2004.

Guinness, Os. *The Dust of Death: The Sixties Counterculture and How It Changed America Forever.* Wheaton, IL: Crossway, 2003.

Herrick, James A. *The Making of the New Spirituality: The Eclipse of the Western Religious Tradition.* Downers Grove, IL: InterVarsity, 2003.

Hunter, George G., III. *The Celtic Way of Evangelism: How Christianity Can Reach the West...Again.* Nashville: Abingdon, 2004.

Lewis, C. S. *The Weight of Glory and Other Addresses.* San Francisco: HarperSanFrancisco, 2001.

Lindsley, Art. *True Truth: Defending Absolute Truth in a Relativistic World.* Downers Grove, IL: InterVarsity, 2004.

Neal, Connie. *What's a Christian to Do with Harry Potter?* Colorado Springs: WaterBrook, 2001.

Schaeffer, Francis A. *The God Who Is There*. Downers Grove, IL: Inter-
Varsity, 1998.

Schaeffer, Francis A. *Pollution and the Death of Man*. Wheaton, IL:
Crossway, 1992.

Stackhouse, John G., Jr., ed. *What Does It Mean to Be Saved? Broadening
Evangelical Horizons of Salvation*. Grand Rapids: Baker Academic,
2002.

Stott, John R. W. *Christian Mission in the Modern World: What the
Church Should Be Doing Now!* Downers Grove, IL: InterVarsity,
1976.

———. *Human Rights and Human Wrongs: Major Issues for a New
Century*. Grand Rapids: Baker, 1999.

Yancey, Philip. *Soul Survivor: How My Faith Survived the Church*. New
York: Doubleday, 2001.

Christian Stewardship of Creation

Beisner, E. Calvin. *Where Garden Meets Wilderness: Evangelical Entry into
the Environmental Debate*. Grand Rapids: Eerdmans, 1997.

Harris, Peter. *Under the Bright Wings*. Vancouver, B. C.: Regent College
Publishing, 2000.

Wilkinson, Loren, ed. *Earthkeeping in the Nineties: Stewardship of Creation*.
Eugene, OR: Wipf and Stock, 2003.

Holistic Christian Living

Bonhoeffer, Dietrich. *Life Together: The Classic Exploration of Faith in
Community*. San Francisco: HarperSanFrancisco, 1993.

Demarest, Bruce. *Satisfy Your Soul: Restoring the Heart of Christian Spirituality*. Colorado Springs: NavPress, 2004.

de Waal, Esther. *The Celtic Way of Prayer: The Recovery of the Religious Imagination.* New York: Doubleday, 1999.

Packer, J. I. *Keep in Step with the Spirit: Finding Fullness in Our Walk with God.* Grand Rapids: Baker, 2005.

Teresa of Ávila. *The Life of Saint Teresa of Ávila by Herself.* New York: Penguin, 1988.

Wicca and Neo-Paganism (by Feminist or Neo-Pagan Authors)

Adler, Margot. *Drawing Down the Moon: Witches, Druids, Goddess-Worshippers, and Other Pagans in America Today.* New York: Penguin, 1997.

Christ, Carol P. *Rebirth of the Goddess: Finding Meaning in Feminist Spirituality.* New York: Routledge, 1998.

Christ, Carol P., and Judith Plaskow, eds. *Womanspirit Rising: A Feminist Reader in Religion.* San Francisco: HarperSanFrancisco, 1992.

Crowley, Vivianne. *Principles of Witchcraft.* San Francisco: Thorsons, 1997.

Cunningham, Scott. *The Truth About Witchcraft Today.* St. Paul: Llewellyn, 2002.

Curott, Phyllis. *Witch Crafting: A Spiritual Guide to Making Magic.* New York: Broadway, 2002.

Frost, Gavin, and Yvonne Frost. *The Magic Power of White Witchcraft.* Paramus, NJ: Prentice Hall, 1999.

Gadon, Elinor W. *The Once and Future Goddess: A Sweeping Visual Chronicle of the Sacred Female and Her Reemergence in the Cultural Mythology of Our Time.* San Francisco: HarperSanFrancisco, 1989.

Gardner, Gerald B. *High Magic's Aid.* Hinton, WV: Godolphin House, 1996.

———. *The Meaning of Witchcraft.* York Beach, ME: Red Wheel/Weiser, 2004.

———. *Witchcraft Today.* New York: Kensington, 2004.

Kelly, Aidan A. *Crafting the Art of Magic, Book I: A History of Modern Witchcraft, 1939–1964.* St. Paul: Llewellyn, 1990.

RavenWolf, Silver. *Teen Witch: Wicca for a New Generation.* Minneapolis: Llewellyn, 1998.

Spretnak, Charlene, ed. *The Politics of Women's Spirituality: Essays on the Rise of Spiritual Power Within the Feminist Movement.* New York: Doubleday, 1982.

Starhawk. *Dreaming the Dark: Magic, Sex and Politics.* Boston: Beacon Press, 1997.

———. *The Spiral Dance: A Rebirth of the Ancient Religion of the Great Goddess, 20th Anniversary Edition.* San Francisco: HarperSanFrancisco, 1999.

———. *Webs of Power: Notes from the Global Uprising.* Gabriola Island, B. C.: New Society, 2002.

Valiente, Doreen. *An ABC of Witchcraft: Past and Present.* Blaine, WA: Phoenix Publishing, 1984.

———. *Rebirth of Witchcraft.* Blaine, WA: Phoenix Publishing, 1989.

Wicca, Neo-Paganism, and Feminism (by Christian Authors)

Barger, Lilian Calles. *Eve's Revenge: Women and a Spirituality of the Body.* Grand Rapids: Brazos Press, 2003.

Hailson, Donna F. G., Catherine Clark Kroeger, Aída Besançon Spencer, and William David Spencer. *The Goddess Revival.* Grand Rapids: Baker, 1995.

Hawkins, Craig S. *Witchcraft: Exploring the World of Wicca*. Grand Rapids: Baker, 1996.

Keyes, Mardi. *Feminism and the Bible*. Downers Grove, IL: InterVarsity, 1999.

Mathewes-Green, Frederica. *Gender: Men, Women, Sex, Feminism*. Ben Lomond, CA: Conciliar Press, 2002.

ORGANIZATIONS

A ROCHA, *http://en.arocha.org*, is an international Christian conservation organization.

C. S. LEWIS INSTITUTE, *www.cslewisinstitute.org*, is committed to challenging, educating, and discipling those who will, like C. S. Lewis, articulate, defend, and live faith in Christ through personal and public life.

THE DAMARIS PROJECT, *www.damarisproject.org*, is an organization in dialogue with feminist spirituality in light of the teaching and life of Jesus Christ.

L'ABRI FELLOWSHIP, *www.labri.org*, has Christian study centers in Europe, Asia, and America where individuals seek answers to questions about God and the significance of human life.

SPIRITUAL COUNTERFEITS PROJECT, *www.scp-inc.org*, is a think tank and evangelical ministry focused on the occult, neo-Paganism, New Age, and cults. The SCP Access Line for counseling services is 510-540-5767.

AUDIO RESOURCES

Lindsley, Art. *The Growing Influence of Neo-Paganism: A Response.*
McLean, VA: C. S. Lewis Institute. Available in cassette. To order, call 1-800-813-9209.
Lindsley, Art, and Catherine Sanders. *The Da Vinci Code Decoded.*
Arlington, VA: C. S. Lewis Institute. Available in cassette. To order, call 1-800-813-9209.

Reader's Guide

Chapter 1

1. On which basic beliefs do Wiccans agree?
2. What is it about witchcraft that draws so many visitors to Salem on Halloween?
3. Why do spiritual seekers look for a religion that is "real"? Is your faith real to you? Why or why not?
4. What do you think of Marisa's view of evil?

Chapter 2

1. How do you feel about the Techno Cosmic Mass? Are you offended? frightened? sympathetic to those who attended? Explain.
2. Do you think the behavior of the Christians in Orange County was appropriate? Why or why not?
3. Are Wiccans to be admired for not being apatheists? Why or why not?
4. In what ways are Wiccan critiques of the church fair and in what ways are they unfounded?

Chapter 3

1. What signs of Wicca do you see in American culture today?
2. Discuss why the Harry Potter series and books based on Wicca are so popular.

3. Should parents be concerned about their children reading books based on Wicca? Why or why not?

4. Discuss ways parents can engage in constructive dialogue with children who are drawn to Wicca because of the Internet, popular entertainment, and books.

5. In what ways is commercialization good for spirituality and religion? In what ways is it damaging?

Chapter 4

1. Why does the idea of a Goddess resonate with the women described in this chapter?

2. Why does a myth not have to be true to be meaningful?

3. Discuss Margot Adler's May Day experience and Peggy Orenstein's story. Why is ritual important to women? What rituals do you enjoy participating in, if any? Should rituals marking life's passages be more honored in the West? by the church? Why or why not?

4. We are created to live in community, yet our Western culture encourages us to live as individuals. What are some ways you can better honor the passages of life in the lives of those in your church, your family, and your community?

5. Who in your life is hardest to love or understand? In light of Carol's and Roberta's stories, what are some ways you can show love to that person?

Chapter 5

1. Does Mary Daly have a right to be angry with the church for its treatment of women? Why or why not? What do you think of her response to Lilian?

2. Why do you think women's bodies are so objectified in Western culture?

3. Do you agree with Mardi Keyes that human dignity comes from being created in the image of God? What are the potential pitfalls of viewing dignity as coming from within?

4. When has the church's treatment of women been consistent with Jesus's treatment of women? When has it been inconsistent?

5. Why did Teresa of Ávila, Catherine of Siena, and some early feminists see the gospel as liberating for women?

Chapter 6

1. What are the main reasons teenagers are drawn to Wicca?

2. What about Christianity turns young people off? How can Christians be better messengers of the gospel?

3. What pitfalls come with deriving your moral compass from a religion that is "malleable," that lets its practitioners add or subtract elements at will?

4. On what basis does Scott say Wicca is unbiased and tolerant? How might his surprise about the booth that promotes ritual sex, whips, and chains challenge his appreciation of Wiccan beliefs?

5. As the students at the New England Catholic prep school learned, Goddess spirituality encourages women to recognize the power within themselves. What are the pros and cons of this belief?

6. What advice would you give a concerned parent of a Wiccan teen?

Chapter 7

1. Why is neo-Paganism flourishing on college campuses?
2. Why is spiritual authenticity important to young adults?
3. Meg consults her gods and goddesses throughout the day. What is she seeking?
4. Margaret Ann experienced two types of behavior from Christians when she abandoned her faith in favor of Wicca. What would have been your response? (Be honest!) How does reading Margaret Ann's story affect your view of Wicca and Christianity?
5. What do Mark Noll, Cathleen, and Margaret Ann have in common?
6. What was Jesus's approach to people? What can we learn from him?

Chapter 8

1. What motivates people to bring neo-Paganism into the Christian church?
2. Do you sympathize with Sue Monk Kidd? Has she arrived at the answer to her problems? Why or why not?
3. What happens when churches neglect the Holy Spirit?
4. Jesus showed keen interest in the lives of those he encountered. Why do many in the West not believe that God still cares about the details of our lives?
5. How can Celtic Christian practices help Christians reach the West with the gospel message?

Chapter 9

1. Why are Wiccans and Pagans involved in the antiglobalization movement?

2. Why do you think many evangelicals have shied away from environmental causes?

3. Does Christianity or Paganism provide a stronger moral basis for creation care? Why?

4. How important is community to you? In what ways could you become more familiar with the environment? with your neighbors?

5. Why are those most rooted to a place—the poor of the Third World—increasingly rejecting traditional paganism and animism in favor of Christianity?

6. What do you think of A Rocha's mission? In what ways could you practice similar exercises in your community? family? school?

Chapter 10

1. How did Alison's story affect you? How did the message of the gospel provide hope for Alison in a way that Wicca never could?

2. How does Daniel's story inspire you?

3. Do you believe that God is really in control and bigger than any enemy, seen or unseen? Why or why not?

4. What can Christians learn from Wiccans and from what motivates them?

5. In Luke 4:16-30, Jesus said that he came for the poor, the outcast, the brokenhearted, the captive, the blind, and the oppressed. Many of the people who appear throughout the pages of this book have admitted to choosing Wicca out of a wounded spirit or a broken heart. In what ways might Wiccans be considered outcasts? oppressed? What are some practical ways Christians can reach out to them in love?

ABOUT THE AUTHOR

CATHERINE EDWARDS SANDERS is a writer with experience in radio, television, and print journals such as the *Weekly Standard,* the *Washington Times, Insight* magazine, *World* magazine, and *Coastal Living.* She has written for the *McLaughlin Group* and was the producer of *Janet Parshall's America* talk-radio program. Her writing has generated local and national radio and television interviews.